T0065804

ONE IN A MILLION
THROUGH THE
GRACE OF GOD

God's Unknown Soldier

JOHN MATHEWS

WESTBOW
P R E S S®
A DIVISION OF THOMAS NELSON
& ZONDERVAN

This book is a work of non-fiction. Unless otherwise noted, the author
and the publisher make no explicit guarantees as to the accuracy of
the information contained in this book and in some cases, names of
people and places have been altered to protect their privacy.

WestBow Press books may be ordered through booksellers or by contacting:

WestBow Press
A Division of Thomas Nelson & Zondervan
1663 Liberty Drive
Bloomington, IN 47403
www.westbowpress.com
844-714-3454

Scripture taken from the New King James Version® Copyright © 1982
by Thomas Nelson. Used by permission. All rights reserved.

ISBN: 978-1-6642-6317-8 (sc)
ISBN: 978-1-6642-6318-5 (hc)
ISBN: 978-1-6642-6316-1 (e)

Library of Congress Control Number: 2022906601

Print information available on the last page.

WestBow Press rev. date: 05/25/2022

Dedication

First of all I dedicate this book to my grandchildren Michael and Peter, who showed great interest in knowing my life history.

Second, I dedicate this book to various individuals, who suggested and encouraged me to write down my life story and testimony. Without their suggestion, I would not think of writing this.

Third, I dedicate this book to my beloved wife, Chinnamma, who shared 47 years of her life with me and stood with me in all my endeavors and activities and was a main reason for my colourful life.

Fourth, but above all, I dedicate this book to my Lord and Savior Jesus Christ, who made all these things possible.

John Mathews.

CONTENTS

ACKNOWLEDGMENTS

I would like to thank my friend Suja George who helped me with the initial formatting and type setting of the manuscript.

I also want to thank my grandnephew, Elson Abraham, who assisted me with the digital proof reading and technological support.

I greatly appreciate and thank Dr. Sajan Mathews, who very kindly wrote a beautiful Foreword for my book.

I would like to acknowledge my deep gratitude to the WestBow team of Editors and design team for their excellent editing and design work. I also want to thank the coordinators, publishing and marketing consultants for their outstanding work and cooperation.

Above all, I thank the Almighty God, who allowed and enabled me to write this book for the benefit of many and for His glory.

FOREWORD

The famous tennis player, Boris Becker once said, "An autobiography is not about pictures; it's about the stories; it's about honesty and as much truth as you can tell without coming too close to other people's privacy." In Psalm 34:8, we read, O taste and see that the Lord is good: blessed is the man that trusts in Him. In this autobiography, a collection of memoirs, dear V. J. Mathews uncle has masterfully combined many touching stories of his life's journey while making sure to tell that God is good and that God always receives the praise and glory. Starting from his birth, childhood, early education, blushing experiences with girls, and stories of his employment in Mumbai, Doha, and US, he is a living example that our God is a prayer answering God, is no respecter of persons, and One who honors those who honors Him. There is seldom a person from India among the Brethren who has held such high and enviable positions with the UK Government, met and interacted with so many dignitaries, national and international, from around the world. Writing this biography in his 70's, his attention to detail is remarkable, his memory is vivid, and his story telling ability is gripping.

In Chapter 3, you'll read about how he met his beloved wife, Chinnamma aunty, and their delayed but exciting union in marriage. In Chapter 6, you'll read about the abundance of God's grace showered upon him in his work despite his high school education, and in Chapter 7, you'll read of V. J. uncle's spiritual life, his ministries, giving, other philanthropic work, along with the 3 CDs recorded, more than 40 songs written, and the many poems he wrote with their titles. All these are evidence of his rich legacy on earth and the even richer deposit the Lord has enabled him to make for eternity. Chapter 8 is full of travel notes of the places he visited around the world, interesting anecdotes, and memories of the people he and aunty met or visited. For those readers who are challenged for time, chapter 10, titled, "In Short" is a summary of the contents of the book. All these are evidence of the remarkable hand of God upon the life of this gracious, honest, hardworking, spiritual, generous, and gentle man of God that God is greatly using even today.

Looking at the amazing blessings of the Lord, undeserving as he says he is, let me conclude with his own words, "I consider myself as One in a Million, or One in Millions, All by the Grace of God."

Dr. Sajan Mathews
Professor of Theology,
Moody Theological Seminary, Chicago
Dec. 2, 2021

PREFACE

After my death, I do not think anybody would venture to write a memoir of my life or my biography. I haven't held any high position and am not famous enough to deserve one. It is also a fact that I never thought of writing an autobiography, but the events in the past few years have changed my thinking. These are the main reasons for that:

1. Before leaving my native place, Ranny, Kerala, India; after selling my house and property there, we arranged a farewell party inviting friends, family, neighbors and members of our church. About 450 people attended that function. During that period, I had the privilege to testify my past life experience and how a mere matriculate (SSLC) was lifted by God and how he blessed me and saved me many times from the mouth of death. After listening to these stories, three or four great men of God suggested that they should be made into a book for the benefit of others and the glory of God's name. I heard that but did not think of doing anything about it.

2. A few years later, my wife, Chinnamma, and I joined a tour group visiting Singapore, Malaysia, and Thailand. The tour, which started in Kerala, India, included forty Malayalees from Kerala. There were Hindus, Muslims, and Christians in the group.

   While in Thailand, we had a long bus journey. The tour guide passed around a microphone and asked us to introduce ourselves. Most people did so in one or two sentences. When my turn came, I said I would need more time, as I wanted to give my life experience and how my God helped me in various situations. My intention was to glorify God's name and proclaim the gospel through my testimony. After

I finished, almost all, irrespective of religion, said that I should make it a book for the benefit of more people. After the bus ride was over, one person came to me and said that he was a counsellor to students who studied abroad and people taking up new jobs abroad. He said that he quoted sayings by Abraham Lincoln, John Mathai (the personal secretary of Indian Prime Minister Jawaharlal Nehru), and so on to encourage them. He agreed that my experience and principles would benefit his students if I published it as a book. I was happy to hear that, but I did not think of writing a book, as I was not a writer.

3. Another time, when we were in India, Saji, my wife's American nephew, hired a minibus and loaded it with his cousins and friends to go to the Wonderla (Veegaland) Adventure Park in Kochi. He asked us to join them, which we did. All of them except me and my wife were Catholics. After an enjoyable day, on our return journey, the youngsters made it more enjoyable by singing and dancing on the bus. After a while, I asked them to stop the celebration. When they all became silent, I said this world and its enjoyment are temporary and vanishing, and none of them would produce permanent peace or happiness. I explained my life experiences and described the peace, happiness, and hope I have as a child of God.

After I spoke, many of them became silent and went into deep thinking. When we reached our destination, Chinnamma and I got out of the bus. Then one by one, all of them came out of the bus and said they would change their attitude and lifestyle. Then they boarded the bus again and went away. At that moment, it struck me that my life experience can change people. But even then, I didn't take any action.

4. Next year, while attending the FIBA conference in the United States, I met an evangelist, who is also a writer, who had attended our farewell party in Ranny. When he saw me, he said, "Sunnychayan, you should meet me when you

come to India next time." He said he would sit with me for a day or two, take some notes, and write a book about me. When I heard that, I thought I should let others know what the good Lord has done in my life, then only His name may be glorified. So, I decided to write down a few important points.

I felt a special inspiration in my mind and began write down these points in detail. Though I am not a writer, and have no previous experience, God gave me a special ability to write down my memories. The next time I went to India, I showed this memoir to Brother K. J. Samuel, a member of our church who is a Malayalam language specialist. After reading through it, he said it was a very good autobiography. But he did not believe many things I said in it, and I had not taken any proof with me. However, I printed out a copy of it and left it there. Still, I did not think of making it a book, and I didn't know how to do it.

One day, quite unexpectedly, Brother Babu K. Varghese and Brother George Koshy, both writers and publishers, visited me at our home in Aluva, Kerala. As they spent some time at my place, I showed them my memoir. Brother Koshy looked through it and said there was enough matter in it for publishing. He also offered to edit it and make arrangements to publish it. I realized that it was God's providence, and I gave him a copy of it for further action.

As things progressed, I wondered how to produce the proof for many inquiries Brother Samuel raised. I prayed to God to solve that problem. After a few days, we went back to America. Let me say it was more of God's providence that Brother Koshy received a visa to attend a conference in the United States.

When he was in New York, I took him home and showed him the documents addressing issues Brother Samuel had raised. A few days later, I received Brother Koshy's edited copy of my story. To my surprise, I saw that other than correcting a few spelling mistakes and changing a few headings, nothing had been changed. I had never even written a small article in my life. I had no higher education or good knowledge of the Malayalam language itself. Moreover, I had left Kerala more than forty years ago and remained out of touch with Malayalam. Yet I found that my language and the style of my writing was good enough to publish a book.

I was very happy and thanked God for making me a writer. He even used me to write a few poems based on biblical characters and a few spiritual songs. I do admit that it is all because of the abundant grace that God has poured upon me. I remember that with a very grateful heart.

Please forgive me for letting the preface go on too long. At the same time, I believe it is better to explain things, so readers will understand these matters well.

I want to clear the confusion some readers might have about my name, which is used differently in different places. I have been known by many names. At home, I was called Sunny. In school, my name was V. J. Mathew. When I took my passport to go to Doha, my name was changed to V. J. Mathews. When I joined the British embassy, as they give emphasis to the first name, they changed my name to John Mathews. When I was in Doha, my friends and church members called me Embassy Sunny. When I immigrated to America, where there is more importance to one's surname, my name was changed to Mathews J. Vettimala. Finally, when I became a US citizen, my name was cut short to John Mathews. As I am known as V. J. Mathews in India, in my poems, songs, and other writings, I use the name V. J. Mathews.

John Mathews
43 Clifton Street, Farmingdale
New York, NY 11735, USA
Home No. 516 420 0752
Cell No. 516 305 3441
E-mail: vjmathews00@yahoo.com

CHAPTER 1

Genesis and Exodus

On September 20, 1985, the fortieth anniversary of the United Nations was celebrated at its headquarters in New York. Presidents, prime ministers, foreign ministers, and even some kings and rulers of the member countries attended. Preparations for the events started many months in advance. Hundreds of FBI agents and New York City police officers secured the hotels where the foreign dignitaries stayed and other places where meetings would be held.

As the date of the anniversary approached, the New York police blocked all the roads and sidewalks within one thousand feet of the UN building. Hundreds of police cars, communication vehicles, ambulances, and fire trucks were all waiting in the vicinity to respond in case of any emergency. On the East River behind the building, two US Navy ships and many police patrol boats moved around. Armed security officers were positioned on the terrace of the UN General Assembly building. Two helicopters flew in the sky above. President Ronald Reagan attended the UN meeting, in addition to the other visiting dignitaries. They all arrived in beautiful motorcades. There were high UN officials and FBI/CID officers waiting at the entrance to receive all the most-respected personalities.

On that day, only UN-invited guests could enter that building, whether you were rich, politically powerful, a foreign ruler, or an American citizen. In these circumstances, I, John Mathews, a simple and ordinary person, son of V. M. John from Ranny, Kerala, walked into this building. I came down from my office on the twenty-seventh floor of One Dag Hammarskjold Plaza, which is situated right in front of the Assembly building. I walked slowly through the gate and into the hall. When the security officers saw the badge that I was wearing, they respectfully led me to my assigned seat. The badge said, "Representative of the British Government."

The UN had issued a very few visitors' passes to major countries. The British UN Mission had received two passes, and the management was good enough to give me one of them. I was the only Indian among the two-hundred-plus British and American staff working in the British government offices in New York.

It was a great privilege for me, an ordinary middle-class man from India, to sit with US President Ronald Reagan, British Prime Minister Margaret Thatcher, Indian Prime Minister Rajiv Gandhi, and many other heads of states to attend the General Assembly meeting for a whole day. It was beyond my expectation and dreams to be with so many great people of the world.

In the morning session, the American president, British prime minister, and the Australian prime minister spoke. At lunch break, I was able to be very near to Ronald Reagan, Rajiv Gandhi, and few other presidents and prime ministers. I had lunch at the executive canteen for delegates and staff in the UN itself. I was back at my designated seat in the afternoon for the second session.

In the afternoon, the Russian Foreign Minister Eduard Shevardnadze started speaking in the Russian language. Even though the translation was there, my attention drifted away and went back to my humble past. I thanked God for bringing me up to this position. After Shevardnadze finished his speech, someone else started speaking. But I could not concentrate because my thoughts went back to my childhood.

My Childhood and Education

I was born as the fourth child of John and Mariamma Vettimala in Angadi, Ranny, Kerala, India. I am told that after having three girls, my mother was praying earnestly for a boy, and then she got me on the seventeenth day of August 1939. (That is equivalent to the Malayalam calendar, 1 Chingam 1115, which is the first day of that year.) Because of my fair color, my mom and sisters used to call me *sayip*, which means "white man." I had one younger sister later. Thus, I became the only son among four daughters. As boys are considered more valuable in India, I was treated as very special among the five children. My parents took very good care of me and brought me up in the best way possible to them.

I have some very good memories of my childhood. Those were good times for our family. Our inner storeroom (*ara*) was always full of paddy (*nellu*, rice), and there were almost always one or two full ripe planters (*vahakula*) hanging there. I used to go in that huge storeroom and sit there and eat until my stomach was full. My mother used to make special sweet snacks (*neyyappum*) every day and feed me. I was even breastfed until the age of four. On our own land, we had different kinds of jackfruit trees, coconut trees, cashew nut trees, and mango trees. Fruits from all these trees were available in plenty.

We had plenty of banana trees. Sometimes, we'd only see the ripe ones when they fell to the ground and birds and squirrels ate them. We had a number of goats, cows, and chickens. Eating eggs, meat, and fruits every day was not available to all people in those days, but we were blessed with plenty of it.

In my younger days, I was interested in watching *karimbattu* (sugarcane processing), oxen cart riding, and paddy field tilling with oxen. Because I was the only son in the family, I was given good food to eat, and I was very strong. My main interest was playing with my friends. But things changed when I turned six and was taken to school. Initially, I didn't like going to school. My mother used to take me by force, sometimes dragging me there. But from class 3 to the end of high school study, I was very punctual and never missed a single day. For some reason, it was very painful for me to miss even one school day.

When I was young, I was very active. I was always climbing onto small trees or rocks. I would sometimes fall off and cause problems for me and others. I had plenty of cane service from my mother. I always irritated my younger sister; she would cry loudly, and my mother would punish me. One day, she had a stick in her hand, and she asked me to stand still for punishing. I ran away from her, and she ran after me. Whenever she was very close to me, she would hit me wherever possible. If I did not run, she would only hit me on my palm. Because of this experience, I never bothered to run away from her when she wanted to punish me.

We had a few coffee plants around our house. One of them was very old. A branch had broken and dried standing straight up. One day, when I was climbing on a branch at the top of that tree, I slipped and fell directly onto this sharp branch. It pierced through my thigh, and I was hanging on it. I cried out loudly, and my mother came running. She picked me up and ran to the doctor a mile away, where I got many stitches and treatments. I was only four at that time. At that time, doctors were not available nearby, and there was no other means of transportation. There was one bus, which used to run through the main road. It went one way in the morning and the other way in the evening.

We used one of our coconut trees for the exclusive use of its tender coconut and sweet water. A ladder was placed on it for my father to get the coconuts. When I was five, I thought I would climb on the ladder and get some coconuts. I had strict orders not to climb on it. But I did, and I reached the top, which was about fifteen feet high. While looking down at my sister in the courtyard, I raised my hand to get a good grip on a leaf stump (*madal*), but unfortunately, I grasped a rotten leaf and lost my balance. The next moment, I was flat on the ground. My parents heard my fall and ran to give me first aid. But there was more damage to my body, and I had to go through months of physical therapy and massages. Luckily, I escaped death because my God miraculously protected me. Praise God.

Another dangerous incident happened in our immediate neighbor's paddy field. Once the harvest is over, they bring all the hay to their land near their house and load it up like a pyramid attached to a tree. We call it *turu*. Two of our neighbors' sons in their mid- to late twenties were stacking it up. They used a *kappi*, a kind of local boom, to raise the hay up. I was around eight years old at that time and watched it with much interest. The two brothers talked to each other, and then one of them asked me if I want to go up. My nature being ready to jump into anything, I said yes. They let me sit on the tip of that long rod and raised me up.

I reached the height of about twenty feet, and suddenly, I fell down. I don't know if they did something purposely to hurt me or whether it was an accident. I could not get up, but nothing broke in my body as I fell on a stack of hay. After a while, I became okay, and the brothers told me not to tell anybody. Fearing further punishment, I did not mention this to anyone (I kept the secret till now). Thank God, I escaped injury or death by the grace of God.

In another incident, there was every chance for me to lose my life if not for God's protection. Just a mile away from our house, there was a large paddy field and a stream running through it, ending up in the big Pampa River. After the harvest, the monsoon rain starts, and these paddy fields often get flooded from six to eight feet of water. In that year, there was a big flooding, and water remained like that for a few days. At that time, elderly people made boats (*changadam*) out of *pindi* (banana tree trunks), joining three or four trunks together, and they'd play in the water using paddles. We children use to stand on high land and watch them.

That day, the older people stopped playing by noon and went to their respective homes for lunch. I was still standing there, along with my older cousin. I was very anxious to get into one of those boats. My cousin asked me if I want to get in, and I said yes. He helped me into one and gave me a good push. The water started flowing slowly toward the stream. I had no paddles to control the boat, and as it moved far away from the land, my cousin got frightened and ran away. But he did not alert anyone.

The boat reached the stream and started moving fast towards the river. I got frightened and started calling out and crying. But no one heard me, as I was far away by then. Luckily, there was a big tree standing with its branches and leaves above the water level at the side of the stream. Praise God, my boat got stuck in its branches, and I hung on there. As I was missing from home for a long time, my father went out with some other neighbors to search for me. Someone said they saw me earlier near the water. They all got so frightened and started calling out loudly for me.

Meanwhile, I stopped crying and started praying. I thought this would be the end of my life, because if the boat dislodged from the tree and reached the river, which was so swollen and moving so fast, it would engulf me in no time. More than two hours passed while I remained stuck on that tree. While I was crying and praying, I saw a wooden boat (*vallom*) coming from the river side and moving in the opposite direction. As it got closer, I shouted with all my might, and luckily, they heard it; they came close, rescued me, and brought me back to the place where I boarded it. By this time, my parents, sisters, and other people had gathered there, and they all thanked God for saving my life.

Sometime later in that summer, the Indian Prime Minister Pandit Jawaharlal Nehru visited our village, Ranny. It was a rare occasion. He was the first prime minister of the independent India. He travelled from Kottayam/Thiruvalla and had to cross the Pampa River to attend a meeting arranged at the high school grounds on the other side of the river. But there was no bridge across the river at that time, and vehicles usually did not cross the river. Luckily, the water level was very low, and the industrious people of Ranny made a temporary crossing with wooden planks and sand, so the prime minister's motorcade could pass through safely. The prime minister was very impressed with this arrangement, and he immediately ordered the state government to build a bridge across the Pampa River.

I am saying all this to come to an interesting thing that happened that day. The motorcade was moving in a walking speed, covered by security, military personnel and thousands of enthusiastic people following them. He was moving in an open car, and many politicians and well-wishers were handing him bouquets and flower garlands. The prime minister, a fair and handsome Kashmiri native, extended his hands out and waved at the crowds.

During this, as a ten-year-old boy, I was following him on one side of the car. I suddenly wanted to touch him. Two or three times, I got very close to the vehicle, but the security agents brushed me aside. As I was very young and because of the big friendly crowd, they didn't see me as a threat. As the car was about to turn into the school, it almost stopped, and Nehru was waving his hand to the people standing on the side. I took this opportunity, squeezed in, and touched his hand. He noticed it and lovingly picked up one of the garlands and gave it to me.

At that moment, I was so happy and felt like I had conquered the world. Later in my life, I had the opportunity to shake hands with chief ministers, prime ministers, and even Queen Elizabeth. I consider all that a blessing from the Lord and thank him for that. No doubt, God is good.

When I was studying in the 5th standard, at leisure time, we children used to play Pandavas and Kaurawas, the legendary enemies. For us, it was a real war. I was the leader of one team; three or four students lifted me up and placed me on their shoulders, and the same with my opponent. We used to fight like hell and many times returned home with a torn shirt or even without one. It was all fun. I remember one time, during lunch time, some of the senior students wanted to apply poison ivy on my body. I was good at running and reached home without giving them a chance to apply it on me. My father came out and scolded them, and then they left.

My mother was a very God-fearing and God-loving person. She was the daughter of an evangelist named Muttootharail Thommachan, who was very close to the British evangelist Noel Sayip and his wife. My mother knew much of the Bible by heart. She used to tell me Bible stories, sing me spiritual songs, and teach me the biblical truths and beliefs. My father had not yet become a believer but later accepted Jesus Christ as his personal Savior; after becoming a child of God, he led a life pleasing unto God, the church, and the community. He later became an elder of the assembly he attended. It was my parents' desire that I also become a child of God.

Because of the desire and prayer of my parents, I had the opportunity to accept Jesus Christ as my personal Savior and become a child of God at the age of ten. On one Sunday, Evangelist Valliyil Mathaichan from Chethakal came to our assembly in Oottupara and took classes for the Sunday school children. On that day, he was able to lead a number of us to the Lord and His salvation.

You can imagine how happy I was of my salvation. Whenever I used to pass through narrow ways and open land, I used to shout out the gospel and sing gospel songs loudly. I used to be number one among the Sunday school students. In those days, I learned by heart the gospel messages preached at meetings and conventions. I have good memories of Brother M. E. Cherian and Brother T. K. Samuel visiting our church and teaching us new songs they had written. Those good memories still linger in my mind.

When Ebenezer English High School started in Ettichuvadu, I joined there in the fourth form (9th standard). I was one of the first batch of students at that school. In the first year, I secured the best student award of the school. It was given to me by Mr. T. M. Varghese, one of the ministers from Kerala. But later, there were some changes among the teachers in our class, and I lost interest; I even missed an anticipated first class in the Secondary School Leaving Certificate (SSLC) final exam.

While I was studying in high school, an interesting incident happened. It is a story of me stoning my own house. Our school was nearly two miles away from my home. There was no bus or any other transportation to school. Every day, we had to walk to and from school. Once the classes finished, we spent time in playing soccer or some other sport. Almost every day, I would come home late. My mother used to warn me every other day and punished me occasionally for coming home late. But my problem was that I didn't want to leave my friends and walk back home alone.

One day, there was a particular need at home, and my mother told me to be back home before it was dark. But we started playing, and I forgot everything and didn't get home until night. My mother was very angry and waited for me with a cane in her hand. As soon as I reached home, she gave me a beating and told me to stand outside of our compound in the walking lane until my father came from work. He would come at least an hour later. In those days, we had no electricity, and as soon as the sun went down, it got dark.

As I stood out there for some time, it was getting very dark, and I became frightened. In those days, people used to tell scary stories about madan, evil spirits walking through the lanes and killing people. I decided that one way or another, I had to get inside the house. Our house had wooden panels on one side. I gathered a few round stones like David and started throwing them at the sides of the house, making big noise. I also shouted out, saying, "If you don't let me in, I will break all those panels."

My mom had no other way, so she asked me to come in, but when my dad came home, she complained to him, and I got punished from him also.

In my last year of high school, the school arranged for an excursion to visit Perunthen Aaruvi, a waterfall a few miles away from the school. It was the first excursion from the school with many students and some teachers. It would be my last opportunity to go on a picnic with my fellow students, as I would be leaving after completing high school that year. So, I was very keen to go on that excursion. But my mom wouldn't let me go. She had her own reasons. First, I was her only son; second, she knew I was sure to jump into some problem in that dangerous waterfall and might even lose my life. So, I could not join my classmates and I was very much disappointed. That disappointment remained with me for a long time. But many years later, after my marriage, I was able to take my parents and Chinnamma to that waterfall and get rid of my disappointment.

After I grew up, I visited so many places around the world with Chinnamma, probably to compensate for the disappointment I had in my younger age. I have a big list of countries and places I visited, and I share that in a later chapter.

During the years I was in high school, I remember the country itself was in a financial crisis. This was after World War II and a newly independent India. Even though we had homegrown foods and vegetables, the hard cash was short. We had four students in school at the same time, and it was difficult for my father to arrange fees for all of us. I remember having paid late fees a few times. I passed my SSLC in the year 1956. At that time, our village had no college, and it was beyond my father's capacity to send me to college far away and pay the college fees, hostel fees, boarding fees, and so on. Therefore, I decided not to go for college education.

In those days, I learned that the Navy was recruiting youngsters for training in Thiruvalla, about thirty miles away from Ranny. So, one day, I took my SSLC certificate and went to the recruiting place. At the first attempt, I was rejected, and I had to come back disappointed. By the time I reached Ranny, it was almost dark. I had to cross a stream, which was very familiar to me. But when I reached its bank, the water was high due to heavy rains. But in order to go home, I had to cross it. I entered the water and moved into the middle of the stream, where the water was very high, and the flow was very fast. I had to lift my dhoti not to get wet. But when I lifted my arms, my school certificate fell into the water (I was holding it in my armpit). I did not notice, as I was struggling to get to the other side in the dark.

When I reached the other side, I realized I had dropped my certificate in the swirling muddy water, which was flowing fast to join the nearby river. The certificate I received after eleven years of study had been lost only two months after receiving it. I was upset and decided not to tell anyone. But I could not hold on to it.

Because of my fear and sorrow, within two days, I got very sick and had a high fever. Finally, as I couldn't contain it within me, I confessed it to a close friend who visited me but asked him not to tell anyone, and he agreed. But within an hour, everyone came to know about it, including my parents. But my father was a man of courage, and he came to me and said, "Don't worry, we will find a solution for it."

Those words soothed me and relieved my fear, and I got over my fever soon. With the efforts of my father, I got a duplicate copy of my certificate. But it is a wonder that I never had to show my certificate to anyone in my whole life, even though I attended many interviews and obtained many jobs. My dear God was good enough to bless me even without the need of an educational certificate. He even blessed me more than my friends and classmates. Praise God for that.

Two of my uncles were in the military, serving in north India, and my brother-in-law worked for Air India in Bombay. When these people came to Kerala on vacation, I used to see them and enjoyed hearing about their luxurious lifestyle. So, from my teenage period, I intended to go to places outside Kerala. The year I completed the high school study, an opportunity came to go to Bombay. The opportunity was not for me but for my father. My second sister was living in Bombay with my elder sister, and the family had a marriage proposal. This marriage was agreed upon and was to be conducted in Bombay itself. So, my father decided to go to Bombay and attend the wedding.

I was keen to go to Bombay and convinced him that it was better if I went. If it was me, I wouldn't have to come back soon, so we could save on the return rail ticket, and I could even look for a job there, it being a big metropolitan city. My father agreed with me, and on December 29, 1956, he let me go to Bombay.

In those days, people living in a village like Ranny didn't wear pants or shoes. We never had *chappels* (sandals), even when we went to school. All the children went to school barefooted and wore dhoti and shirts. Even football games were played barefooted. But my father thought I should have a pair of pants to travel to Bombay and attend the wedding. In those days in Ranny, there was not a single shop that sold ready-made pants.

So, my father, who was a tailor himself, made a pair of pants for me, and I wore it for my travel. It was not a regular item he stitched in the normal line of stitching. I think it was his first-time stitching pants. I traveled to Bombay with the pants on but barefooted. When I reached Bombay, my brother-in-law picked me up at the station and immediately took me to a shoe shop and bought a pair of sandals for me. I started my journey from Aluva, and it took two days to reach Bombay, around 530 kilometers (330 miles) away. It was the first time I travelled in a train. Before that day, the longest distance I had traveled was up to Kottayam, which was about fifty miles away from my home.

CHAPTER 2

Alone in a Great City

When I arrived in Bombay, I felt it was a new world. Wide roads with thousands of cars, colorful taxis, trucks and trains, fast-moving people in the thousands, and bright streetlights made me feel I was in a wonder world. I had never seen anything like this before. The streetlights made night like day, and I was astonished when I compared them with the streetlights in Ranny, where the light barely reached the bottom of the post. From 1956 until 1969, when I left for Doha, Qatar, I trained in Bombay, where I gained the strength and confidence I have today.

When I reached Bombay, I stayed with Thankamma, my elder sister, and her husband in Chembur, a suburb of Bombay. It was called a township colony, where hundreds of three-story buildings were built. There were many Malayalee (Keralites) families in that mixed community from different parts of India. There were people from Ranny itself, and among them was Mr. T. M. Abraham and family, son of evangelist Erumelil Thommachan. Two of his young brothers also stayed with him; we all called him Avarachayan. A small group of Indian Pentecostal church members used to gather at his place every Sunday. Both Avarachayan and his wife, Amminikochamma, were very nice people. They sincerely loved everyone and were very hospitable and caring. Their lives were good examples for me to follow. One of his younger brothers, Simon, was my age, and we used to go to the typewriting institute and other places.

Two days after I reached Bombay, my second sister, Saramma, got married to Mr. P. V. Mathai. He was wearing a full suit, and the wedding and reception were all in Western style. The well-decorated, three-tier wedding cake and a reception with Western music were all new experiences for me. As my brother-in-law was a Navy man, he had his own naval quarters, and they moved to his quarters. After some time, Air India, where my elder brother-in-law worked, opened its new staff colony in Kalina, Santa Cruz, and we moved to beautiful new quarters there.

Before I go further, I want to mention an incident that happened just a week after my arrival in Bombay. This incident frightened and pained our family members and neighbors. From my childhood, I was known for not staying quiet. Always I wanted to do something, even if it was wrong. I was also keen to learn about things personally or directly. When villagers move to Bombay, it is not easy to get adjusted to the fast lifestyle, especially traveling on trains. Many times, you would take the fast train instead of the slow train, and it may not stop at the station you want. You may end up somewhere else and run into a lot of problems, especially, if you don't know the local Hindi or Marathi language.

Another problem is that once the electric train starts, it moves very fast. They have open doors, and if you are standing at the door and extend your head out, there is every chance of hitting your head on the electric posts, which stands very close to the train all the way. There were many cases where new people were knocked out and disfigured or killed. So I had been warned of these things by my sister and brother-in-law, who asked me not to go out alone anywhere until I was trained.

One morning, my brother-in-law went to work. Then Thankamma and I were left alone at home. After lunch, I thought I should go out and see some nearby parts of Bombay. So, I told my sister I would go out and see some places nearby and return home soon. On that condition, she allowed me to go out. Once I got out, I straightaway went to the nearest railway station and bought a ticket for the next station, Kurla. Kurla is a very populated town and a major rail terminal. Immediately, a train arrived at the station going to Victoria terminus via Kurla. I boarded it and got out at Kurla station.

I went out of the station and entered a very crowded and vibrant street market. I walked around, watching the crowd and busy activities there. I kept moving and came to the end of the street. When I came to an open place, I heard very loud roaring sound from nearby. I wondered what it was and decided to check it out. I asked someone, and they said it was the sound of the aircraft testing its engines. I knew that a month or so earlier, Air India had acquired several Boeing 707 planes. They were testing its engines.

I thought if the sound was coming from so close, I should go and see the planes and the airport. Before that, I had never seen an airplane nearby. So I started walking toward the sound. I walked for quite a while, but still it was far away. Then I asked someone, and he said it was miles away. But as I had already walked a lot, I was not prepared to turn back. So I continued walking and finally reached the destination, where I had a glimpse of the gleaming, brand-new 707 aircraft. I was amazed at the size of the plane. Then I saw the terminal building. It was the Tata air works, and it was the arrival and departure terminal. It was a small place, compared to the new Santa Cruz airport terminal that opened a year later.

As I came out from the terminal building, I saw a few luxurious buses lying there and went over to have a closer look. While I was enjoying the opulent buses, someone tapped me on my shoulder. When I looked back, I saw Mr. Sukumaran Nair, who stayed on the ground floor of our building in Chembur; he drove one of those buses for Air India. After a while, he told me he was going to the West End Hotel in the city, to bring some passengers for the London flight. He also told me I could go with him, and once he came back from the city, his duty would be over, and we could go home together.

I was so delighted to hear I could ride on that luxury bus and see the city. So, I gladly accepted the offer. I had been concerned about the thought of walking back to the railway station. So, I thought it was a blessing in disguise.

Enjoying the ride and the side views, we finally reached the hotel. We waited there for quite some time. I was sitting on a seat right in front, near the driver. Around nine o'clock, passengers started coming and taking their seats. All of them were Westerners in their full suits and coats. Sukumaran Nair had on a white uniform. I was wearing just pants, a shirt, and a pair of sandals. When I saw them, I dreamt in my mind that one day, I would also put on suits and travel around on a plane. As more passengers came in, I had to vacate my seat and get out of the bus.

At this point, Sukumaran Nair understood his foolishness. So, he took me aside and explained that he could not say no to a passenger to accommodate me, and he expressed his helplessness. I understood it but was quite a stranger to that part of the city, and I didn't know how to get back home. Especially it was night, and I didn't know the local language. Sukumaran Nair was also concerned and upset, but he was helpless in that situation. Then, he pointed out to me that if I walked for a small distance, I would reach the railway station, and if I took a train to Kurla, I could change to another train that would take me to Chembur station; I could then walk down to the colony. He also did a good thing. Without my asking, he gave me the money for the train fare. Otherwise, I would have been in more trouble, as I didn't have enough money with me. After a while, he drove off in the bus to the airport, full of passengers. I took courage and started walking toward the station.

In the meantime, my sister got upset, as I had not come back as I promised. She informed her dear ones and neighbors, who comforted her, saying that I would come home at any moment. By that time, my brother-in-law also came home from his work. As time passed and night grew tall, fear gripped everybody. People started uttering guesswork. Some said I might have got onto some fast train and ended up somewhere else far away. Someone said an accident might have happened, and I might have passed away. After hearing these comments, my sister started crying, and a commotion started. Then someone suggested they go and search for me.

So about fifteen people went to different directions. Different groups went to nearby police stations, railway stations, hospitals, and the mortuary. In those days, no one had any telephones, cars, bikes, or even a bicycle. They had to personally walk to every place and inquire. Even the different groups couldn't communicate to each other. The people who went to the nearby places came back around eleven o'clock without any good news. Then more people started crying, and some started praying. The people who went to distant places came back by midnight. By that time, Sukumaran Nair finished his duty, and when he came home, he explained what happened. Then people put aside their grief, as they knew the reason for the delay, and they also got some relief from knowing I was alive.

From the West End hotel to the V. T. railway station, I had to pass through a large vacant field. After dark, it's usually under the control of *gundas*, thieves, alcoholics, and beggars. At that time, I didn't know about it, and I encountered a few of them on the way. By the grace of God, nobody troubled me; on the contrary, they gave me directions to the railway station. When I reached the station, I bought a ticket to Chembur. By that time, the rush was over, and there was a direct train to Kurla. So, I took a train to Kurla. I got off at Kurla and enquired about the train to Chembur. It was almost midnight, and I was told there were no more trains until the next morning. He also said there was only one station in between, and if I was not afraid, I could walk through the tracks about a mile. Though I was afraid to walk in the pitch darkness, I thought about my sister and other people who were waiting anxiously for my news. So, I decided to walk all the way down the rail track, all alone, at midnight.

I finally reached Chembur and got back home. I was hungry, sweating, and tired. It was about 1:30 a.m. when I reached my house, where they were tired of crying and praying. When they saw I was safe and sound, they were happy and relieved. Some gave me advice; one person said I was smart, and other people said I wouldn't get lost in Bombay anymore. Thus, that event got over, but it was the grace and care of God that brought me home safe. Praise God.

I lived in Bombay for a little over twelve years. Those days were quite eventful, but I'll only write about a few cases in which I received much grace from God. For the first two years after I reached Bombay, I stayed with my sisters and attended typewriting classes. It was very difficult to get a job in Bombay without a profession. In those days, thousands of Malayalees lived in Bombay without a job, as dependents to relatives and friends.

After studying typewriting for a year, I started going to the Fort area of the city to look for a job. My elder brother-in-law arranged a monthly railway pass for me, so I could take a journey at any time. He also gave me a rupee every morning as pocket money. That one rupee was a big amount in those days. I could have a full South Indian vegetarian lunch for half a rupee, and I used to drink a bottle of Coca-Cola for a quarter rupee (during my stay in Bombay, cold Coca-Cola was my favorite drink).

As jobs were not easy to find, I used my free time to become familiar with every corner of Bombay City. While I was there, I went to Coloba, Nariman Point, Marine Drive, Chowpathy, Hanging Gardens, Gateway of India, Bellard Pier, Victoria Terminus, Crafford Market, Cooperage, Elephanta Cave, Bombay Central, Worli, Church Gate, Boriville National Park, and many other places I have good memories about.

Yes, we were talking about my search for a job. I got into many offices in the Fort area and inquired about job openings. At one of the offices, someone told me about a Malayalee officer called Alexander in the Stanvac Oil Company (now Mobil Oil) who helped many people. I decided to go and see him one day. His office was in a beautiful twelve-story fully air-conditioned building situated between Church Gate and Nariman Point. There were very few such fully air-conditioned offices in Bombay at that time.

As I entered the building, I felt like shivering, as it was very cold. The receptionist was a modern young woman who was well-dressed, well-mannered, and beautiful. When I said I wanted to see Mr. Alexander, she contacted him on the intercom, got his permission, and showed me the way to his office on the upper floor. He received me very gracefully and asked about my qualifications, experience, and where I lived in Kerala.

Then he very gracefully told me there were no openings there that could fit me and wished me good luck. I realized it was very difficult to get a job in such a nice company with just a high school education. Though I didn't get a job there, I liked the status and standard of working in such an office and prayed to God to let me also have such opportunity in the future. The good Lord heard my prayer and, later in my life, provided me with all the status, position, and luxury offices I asked for. That is why I am writing this story, to say that my Lord is good.

Later, while I was in an office searching for a job, I met a charted accountant who had his own auditing company. He asked me to go and see him in his office. I went and interviewed with him; he was pleased with me and hired me as an apprentice with him. I worked with him for six months. It was my first job, and the salary was fifty rupees a month. His office was in Kalbadevi, an exclusive area of Gujaratis. The narrow roads were always filled with cars, carts, and people. In addition, there were a number of huge cows walking around in the middle of the road. Nobody was bothered about them, and nobody would move them from the road to the sides. They consider the cow as one of their gods.

An incident happened while I was working in Kalbadevi. I was sent to deliver some documents to a company in Worli. After that, I was to take a train from the nearby Parel rail station to go back to the office. It was not far to the station, and I decided to walk, instead of taking a bus. As there were no sidewalks, I walked in the road, which was risky due to vehicle traffic. There was a vast empty field on one side of the road, and I decided to walk through the field. As it was wide open, I ran down and jumped to the lower level without any problem. After a while, another lower level came, and I jumped without paying any attention.

But as soon as I landed, I realized that I had jumped into a simmering heap of fire. On realizing the danger, I immediately jumped away and escaped having my clothes catch on fire. But during the course, one of my sandals fell into the fire, and the one on my other foot was burned and lost its shape due to the heat; I had to throw it away. After I escaped from the fire, I looked back and realized that it was a place where the municipalities dumped the city waste and burned it. It had burned out, and only a small portion was simmering under the ash. If my pants had caught fire, I would have perished in that deserted place without any help. My good God delivered me miraculously from a fiery death.

I walked up to the station without any shoes or sandals. I felt ashamed to travel barefooted on the train. I didn't have enough money to buy sandals or take a taxi to the office, which was very far. So, I sat down on a chair on the platform and waited there until night; I went back home without anyone noticing my bare feet. So, on that day, my great God saved me from another possible disaster.

No one who comes to Bombay escapes from the illness of chickenpox. Three years after my arrival in Bombay, I also got it. At that time, I was staying in a boarding house in Ville Parley. After my symptoms showed up, one of my fellow boarders took me by train to Arthur Road Hospital, which treated these kinds of contagious diseases. I had body pain and a fever. As there was no way of informing any of my relatives, no one visited me during my fifteen-day stay there. But a day after I was admitted, I met another Malayalee patient, who happened to be from my own village. He was from a rich family in Ranny, and he was a very jolly and funny person. He was a very smart and handsome young man. The whole day, he would keep me entertained with his jokes and fairy tales of his lifestyle and the large amount of money he spent. I believed all that, as I knew he was from a rich family. He took me into a different world, and therefore, I didn't feel any harshness of the chicken pox during those fifteen days. Before we got discharged, he took the details of my work, the date on which my salary was paid, and the address of my boarding place.

On the first day of the next month, the salary day, when I reached my hostel after work, I saw him waiting for me there. After a few initial comments about my welfare, he spoke of great things and another world. Then suddenly, he asked me for about 250 rupees. He said he needed it for some urgent purpose and would return it in a day or two.

I was surprised when he asked me for money. His expensive clothes, fair color, and handsome body declared to anyone that he was a rich man. And it was true. I felt ashamed, as I could not give him all that he asked. But I gave him 150 rupees, which was a major part of my salary. He said he would see me soon and walked away. A few months later, I met some other people from Ranny and inquired about this person. They told me he had taken money from many people and had never returned anything to anybody. Now after more than fifty years, I have never seen him again, and my money has not been returned. But I learned a lesson.

But there were many good people who loved me and cared for me. One among them was Brother Varghese, who worked at the Aarey Milk Colony. He knew me as he was a friend of my elder brother-in-law. While I was working as an apprentice in Kalbadevi, Brother Varghese managed to get me at typist clerk position in Indian Plastics, a Birla company, in Kandivali. After working in the office there for a year, I was appointed head of the Packing and Dispatching Department of the radio manufacturing division of the company. There were a number of people working under me as packers and dispatchers. This was a position even long experienced people did not get.

With my new position, I was friendship with production managers, sales managers, and administrative officers. A year went by in a very successive manner. In those days, one of our major distributors, Standard Radio Company, opened a fully air-conditioned sales room in the newly opened Maratha Mandir. The owner of Standard Radio Company told our administrative officer he was looking for a smart and reliable person who could take full charge of the showroom and its stock and sales. Without any doubt or hesitation, he recommended my name. That's after two years of service in the Birla company.

I joined Standard Radio Company as the salesman in charge of the showroom. For a short period, the proprietor and his two sons used to be there with me all the time. But as time passed and they gained confidence in me, the entire showroom was fully entrusted to me. Even the main key was given to me to open and close the showroom. Thus, I became fully in charge of the showroom, though one of his sons remained with me to assist me, and the proprietor used to visit the office when he was free.

That showroom was fully air conditioned, and as a salesman, I was always well dressed, with a suit and tie. So, within four years of my prayer at the Stanvac office, my prayer had come true. Thank God for that.

A few years later, Standard Radio Company lost its sole

distributorship for Jhankar Radio, and business in the showroom started declining. The future of the business was bleak, and the proprietor, Mr. M. H. Mehta, was very concerned about my future. Therefore, he gave me a letter addressed to Mr. Fazalboy, the managing director of General Radio and Appliances, and asked me to go and see him. After he read the letter, he asked me to come and join his firm as soon as I left the other job. He also introduced me to the manager and the head of the large showroom they had.

Next month, I joined the new place as a salesman. This company was a part of the Tata organization. They used to deal with so many products like radios, radiograms, cooking ranges, pressure cookers and other kitchen appliances, air conditioners, public address equipment, and medical equipment. This was the biggest electronic appliances and equipment showroom in Bombay. There were many employees and nearly a dozen salesmen in the showroom. One of my high school classmates worked in the accounts section. I worked there for more than four years. Later, I also had the opportunity to work as a sales representative for the same firm.

While I was working there, I had the opportunity to deal with many high officials, dignitaries, cinema stars, police and military officers, and several foreigners. Due to that, I developed the experience and confidence to handle responsible matters. They even used to send me to trade exhibitions to man our stalls. Thus, I gained more self-confidence in myself, and the company recognized my ability, responsibility, and faithfulness.

There are some interesting incidents that happened during my high school period and working in Bombay. One incident happened when I was studying in the 11th standard. I usually brought my lunch from home and ate it, along with other friends, sitting at a small restaurant nearby. Some days, when I didn't bring lunch from home, I bought something from the restaurant and ate it there. Also, in the evening, on our way back home from our sports activities, we would go to this restaurant and finish up all the unsold items there. The owners of the restaurant were very pleased with us, and the owner's wife used to call me son, affectionately.

Though I was short in stature, I was very strong for my age. One afternoon, after we finished our lunch, a young man came in. He was about thirty years old. Though not very tall, he was very athletic, with big muscles and a shapely body. At first look, we all thought he was a *fileman,* or an athlete. In fact, he was a fileman who came there to teach *gusti* or nadan fighting to a group of people in the area. With the intention of popularizing himself or attracting more students, he stood outside and challenged us. He said he was teaching gusti and would like to prove it, if anyone dared to fight with him.

There were older and bigger boys amongst us, but no one dared to fight with him. I couldn't bear his challenge and said I would fight with him. When he heard this, he was very happy because he knew he could defeat me easily. So, he stood there and prepared to face me. My friends and the lady from the restaurant tried to stop me, saying he was very strong and dangerous. But I decided to go ahead and stood in front of him. He was standing there showing his muscles and standing in a fighting pose. One of the boys shouted, "1, 2, 3," and within a second, before he could catch me, I moved behind him and with one move caught him by his hip, lifted him, and threw him to the floor.

When all the schoolchildren saw this, they shouted at the fileman and belittled him. He became very angry, got up, and tried to catch me, saying he would kill me. By that time, I ran into the restaurant, and the owner's wife shut me in a room. Not only that, but all the children also stopped him from entering the restaurant. Though he made a big scene there and asked her to release me, she did not, and the children shouted back, saying nobody wanted to learn gusti from him. For the next period of classes, the boys escorted me to the class. Within a week, everybody in that area came to know about it, and the fileman closed his classes and left the place, as he lost his credibility.

Another incident happened in Bombay, when I was working in Maratha Mandir Showroom. One of my friends from school was working in Gujarat for two years. When he came to Bombay on vacation, he came to see me. It was lunchtime, and I was all alone in the office. After my friend came in, I locked the door, and we started talking. He had learned some defensive and offensive steps and some gusti. He told me he could get a lot of milk in Gujarat, and he used to drink a lot of it and became very strong. He also showed me some defensive and offensive steps.

I couldn't stand it for long. So, I stood up and asked for his hand. He extended his hand to me; I caught hold of it, pulled him towards me, moved behind him, and caught him in his hip area. I lifted him and threw him to the floor. As the floor was carpeted, not much damage was done. But he never again boasted about his strength and gusti to me.

When I was working at General Radio and Appliances, another incident happened. As I mentioned earlier, there were many people working there. People were from different states like Gujarathi, Marathi, Sindhi, Goa, and Keralite. In addition to me, there were four more other Keralites working there. We young Keralites often went to lunch as a group and had a great time together.

In this incident, after a heated argument, a Gujarathi co-worker and I were involved in a fist fight that landed him in the local hospital and a complaint sent to the local police station but no case was filed against me as I had some influence in that station. He was also released from the hospital after a day or two. Luckily, it ended up without any serious consequences.

While I was in Bombay, I fell sick a few times. Once, I was infected with yellow fever. It became so severe that my skin itself turned yellow. I did not know it, but someone told me. Then I became bedridden, but my elder brother-in-law brought me some *ottamooly*, special country medicine. I became well within no time. But after taking that medicine, I was told not to eat chicken for a few months. I did not follow this instruction and ate chicken, and due to that, even now I have some jaundice symptoms in my blood.

The second time, I had a severe fever. I was very tired and bedridden at home. My sister and brother-in-law were not there, and as I was too sick, I could not go to the doctor. At that time, I was staying on the first floor of an Air India building. As I was lying down, I looked out through the window and saw two nuns wearing white clothes walking through the side of the opposite building. After a while, they came in near my bedside, prayed for me, and went away. Within a short time, my fever came down, and I felt completely well. I do not know how they came to know about my sickness or who opened the door for them. Also, I have not heard of nuns going around houses and praying for sick people.

Later, I told Thankamma about it, but she said she had not seen any nuns or opened the door for them. I believe, in my helpless condition, the good Lord sent His angels and healed my sickness. Praise the Lord for that.

In another incident, I could have lost my life, but my good Lord protected me. I used to go to work by taking a bus from home to Santa Cruz railway station and then take a train. Once those electric trains started, they moved very fast. And because of overcrowding, they never closed the train doors. People would hang on to something while the train ran. There were electric posts standing on both sides of the rail, and if you hung over by an inch, you could hit the post and die. Many people, especially newcomers who are ignorant of this danger, died from these accidents. The fast trains that come from Virar or Borivali always came overcrowded, and people in Santa Cruz never got a chance to get on during the morning rush hour. Though I had a first-class pass, I never could get inside the train.

On that day, the train came, and as usual, I caught hold of the side rod and hung on, with one hand and one leg on the edge of the door board. In those days, I used to attend evening college, and I had two thick textbooks in my other hand. As the train started moving and picked up speed, I realized I was hanging out too much and tried to squeeze in a bit, but I could not. The train was almost halfway through the platform, and in another second or two, I would hit the electric post, and that would be my end.

I had to make a split-second decision. In my mind, I asked God to help me and let go of the hand grip. I fell onto the platform and kept rolling because of the speed of the train. Immediately, the passengers standing on the platform caught me and saved me from rolling onto the rails. My books and everything flew away. I had some bruises and cuts on my hands, legs, and face. My shirt and pants got stained with blood. Some people told me to go to the hospital, but I caught a taxi and went home. When Thankamma saw me back home with blood everywhere, she started crying and asked what happened. I explained everything to her, and we both praised God for miraculously saving my life. I did not go to work for the next two days.

We used to open the Maratha Mandir showroom on Sundays. As I was in charge of the showroom, I had to be there every Sunday. Because of the showroom hours and Sunday opening, I could not attend any worship meetings or any other spiritual activities. On top of that, because of the urging of Kaku Bhai, the son of the proprietor, who was my age, I started going to Hindi and English movies to keep him company. Pentecostals don't allow watching movies. The pastor and some other brothers reminded me of the importance of attending church. But due to these circumstances, I could not go to church. Gradually, I became a backslider and completely avoided church for a few years. In between, I received one or two marriage proposals from Brethren families through my father. As I had been going to a Pentecostal church since my arrival in Bombay, I did not agree to any of those proposals.

At that time, my third sister, Annamma, got married in Kerala, and I was able to attend. Her husband, Mr. E. M. Matthew, was from Mallapally, Kerala. He was a railway officer in north India. After the marriage, he got transferred to Bombay, and they lived in Powai. After a few years, he left his railway job and decided to serve God as an evangelist. He had two children and worked very hard for the Lord. He completed his task and joined his heavenly Father in 2006.

CHAPTER 3

$\infty\!\infty\!\infty$

A Family for the Lonely Person

My close friend Achankunju got married in those days, and two or three of my coworkers also got married. Then I got an inclination that I should do the same, but certain incidents that happened in my earlier life kept me from searching for my life partner. One of them happened when I was very young. I was about three years old. A poor family that was staying in our own land had a young girl about two or three years old. She used to spend much of her time in our house, as her mother worked in our house, helping my mother. One day, before my mother gave me a bath, she put oil all over my body, and I was walking around naked. This young girl came there by chance, and she got curious about what was hanging in front of me, and she came over and had a close look at it. I think she also probably touched it. When my elder sister came and saw this, she scolded us. Not only that, but she also told the other members of my family, and she started calling me the girl's name. Whenever we used to fight each other, she used to call me the girl's name. This went on till I finished my schooling and went to Bombay.

Another incident happened when I was about fifteen. My father sent me to get money from a man who owed it to him. He lived nearly a mile away from us. When I reached there, I saw a young girl about seventeen standing outside their house and acting funny; she focused her attention to one side. I observed her for a while and thought there was something wrong with her. It looked like she was expecting somebody.

Just then, I decided to do something stupid. I quietly moved behind her and covered her eyes with both of my hands. She got startled and was frightened as she looked at me, as she had never seen me before. But before she cried out, I told her who I was and said I came to get money from her father. She told me no one was at home, and she would give the message to her father when he came. Then I went back home. But her boyfriend was sitting in the branches of a big mango tree and watching everything that happened. She was sending him a message with those actions. After a few days, my father scolded me and warned me not to repeat such things. The girl's boyfriend had told everything to my father. Then I realized that all girls were troublemakers.

The next memory is a sweet one from my teenage years. I went to the Ebenezer English High School to register for the fourth form (that is 9th standard). When I went there, I saw a sweet young girl in the principal's office. I had to wait there for a while, and two or three times, our eyes met, and I felt something in my mind. Later, when the school opened, I found out she was a student in my class. My strange feelings turned out to be love. From her looks and behavior, I realized that she also liked me.

Within a few months, she captured my whole heart, and I used to spend day and night just thinking about her. Because we both were comparatively shorter than the other students, we sat in the front row, facing each other. Even when the teacher was instructing us, we used to look into each other's eyes and find happiness. Whenever there was a function at the school, we made sure to sit where we could see each other.

This girl was from a rich family, and though a Christian, she was from a different denomination. I knew it would be difficult for us to join together, as nobody would agree to it. But as months passed by, our minds were getting closer. In those days, boys had no freedom to talk to an unrelated girl in public. In addition, I had no opportunity to see her alone or talk to her. Once the classes were over, she went in one direction, and I went in another, as our residences were in the opposite areas. Her elder sister, younger brother, and two cousins also went to the same school. So, I never had the opportunity to tell her I loved her. If any of them knew I was after her, there was every chance for me to be in trouble. Therefore, we loved each other silently for nearly three years, till we both finished high school.

After high school, she went to college, and I went to Bombay. Even after reaching Bombay, I thought about her for another two years, suffering the pain of separation. I feel sorry for myself when I remember those days, as at that time, I did not have the courage to tell her I loved her, and I didn't know how serious she was, as we never had the opportunity to talk to each other. However, later, I realized that it was only a teenage attraction, and she had not taken it seriously.

Because I had such a discouraging background, I was reluctant to get involved with girls for a long time. Then as my friends were having girlfriends and even getting married, I thought I should display my courage and show my manhood. One day, I was visiting my cousin, who worked as a nurse in a hospital. There, I came across a beautiful girl. My cousin introduced her to me, and we gradually fell in love. We remained friends and lovers for a year. Although we were lovers, we only talked on the public phone once or twice a week and met together for a few minutes once in a month or so. I never even had a chance to take her to the cinema. Once, when we were together, she acted like she wasn't a right match for me. I told her we should end our relationship, and our love affair ended there. I never saw her again.

In those days, many people went to the Arabian Gulf and Africa to find work. I saw some of my friends coming on leave with lots of money and a number of foreign items not available in India at that time. My friend Achankunju and I had an uncontrollable desire to go to the Persian Gulf or the United States. As we didn't find any way to go, we started praying to God and attending some special services in a well-known church in Mahim. We believed that the good Lord would open a way for us.

One day, I met a girl named Chinnamma. She had gone to nursing school with Achankunju's wife, Mariamma. Because I had the bad experience with another nurse, I didn't think I would marry a nurse. But when I observed her humility, open-mindedness, and other behavior, I was attracted to her. One way or other, I felt some closeness to her. On another occasion, when we met at a common friend's place, we were talking about weddings, and I expressed my views and expectations of a wife. Chinnamma expressed similar views and expectations of a husband.

Later, we found out that my thoughts and Chinnamma's thoughts were very matching and complementary. Except for the difference in our church beliefs (she was Catholic), everything else was in favor for us to get married. So, one day, I mentioned this to Chinnamma, and she said if I was willing, she was also interested in it. But she said as she was Catholic, the marriage had to be conducted in a Catholic church. As I was still backsliding from our church, I thought it wouldn't be a big problem. So, it moved into a wedding proposal. I told her that I liked her, but I had to get my family's approval. She agreed to that.

Luckily, my three sisters and their husbands and Ammachi, my mother, were all in Bombay. As agreed, I brought Chinnamma to my elder sister's house one day. They all met Chinnamma and talked to her, and they liked her very much. We all agreed to go ahead with the proposal, and my photo and personal details were given to Chinnamma to be sent to her parents. Chinnamma's photo and family details were sent to my father in Kerala. Approval from both families in Kerala came soon. We decided to conduct the official engagement before Ammachi left for Kerala. As if it was God's will, everything went well, and our engagement took place in Bombay; we decided to conduct the wedding in six months' time in Bombay.

But within a month after our engagement, Chinnamma received job offers from the gulf and the United States. She had been applying there for a while. Interviews and other procedures had already taken place a few months ago. The appointment order and air tickets came first from the gulf, so she rejected the US offer and took the job in the gulf. Some of her friends accepted the US offer and moved to America. One condition in the contract was that applicants must be unmarried. They could marry after completing the two-year contract. So, our wedding was postponed for two years. At the end of 1966, Chinnamma boarded the plane to take up the position of a staff nurse in the Ministry of Public Health in the Emirate of Qatar.

For the next two years, I suffered a lot of separation pain (*viraha dukkam*). In those days, there were no phone connections with Qatar. The only consolation was the biweekly letter I received from Chinnamma. It was nice to read about her friends, duty, and lifestyle there. Also, it was different from India. After one year, she started writing about the wedding, asking when, where, and how. As decided earlier, we wanted the wedding to take place in Bombay. As she was Catholic, the wedding must be conducted in a Catholic church. In order to get permission for our marriage, I had to go through some classes to learn the rules, regulations, and teachings of the Catholic church. I did that and obtained the permission. As directed by Chinnamma and agreed by both of us, I booked the date, the church, the priest, the reception place, and so on. The invitation cards were printed, and I invited our friends, family, and relatives. The order for the party was given, and I booked a limousine, a white Impala. Arrangements for photography were also made. An expensive wedding suit was prepared for me.

In short, I made preparations for a grand wedding in the city of Bombay. It was both our wish to have a grand wedding, and Chinnamma guided me through her letters. According to the plan, she would fly to Bombay, stay there for a day, and then go to Kerala, returning to Bombay after ten days, along with her brother and four other cousins. I also arranged to bring my father and his younger brother, and one of my uncles from Kerala for the wedding. I booked hotel and food and local transportation arrangements for all of them for a period of two weeks.

While making all these arrangements, I had a certain amount of tension and concern in my mind. There were several reasons for that. First of all, in those days, air travel was not as safe and frequent as today. I was concerned if she would arrive safely on time. Second, even if she arrived safely, I didn't know if she would change her mind. I was aware of some cases like that. In those days, many nurses who had made wedding promises to their longtime boyfriends had gone away to work in the gulf or the United States. Within two or three years, their status changed, and they came back with lots of money, gold, and so on. Then they decided to marry someone else, as the family suggests, according to their present status. Some girls even do it without the knowledge of their longtime boyfriends.

Such thoughts and doubts had crept into my mind. But I regained courage and arranged everything as we planned. By the grace of God, Chinnamma arrived safely in Bombay as planned. She brought expensive gifts to give all my sisters and brothers-in-law, even before the wedding, without my telling her. They were all very happy and pleased with her. The next day, she left for Kerala and returned to Bombay within ten days.

In the meantime, my father and the other dear ones also arrived in Bombay. Thus, our blessed wedding took place on October 20, 1968, at Saint Michael's Church in Mahim, Bombay. Even in those days, we had flower girls, a best woman, and a best man for our wedding. The reception and everything went well, and we were very pleased. There were about four hundred guests consisting of family, friends, coworkers, and neighbors.

Two strange things happened in connection with our wedding. First, someone I brought from Kerala, paying train fare and providing free accommodation and free transportation, did not enter in the church to witness my wedding. It was not because he was against me, but because of his opposition to the Catholic religion. Second, while we all were traveling together back to Kerala in the train, he told me in front of Chinnamma that I should not have married a nurse. The funny part is that one of his two daughters studied nursing and became a nurse later. Not only that, but he also had five sons and arranged all their marriages, to five nurses. This is the world.

I fully believe that our marriage was according to the will of God, and I thank God for providing Chinnamma to me. Our good Lord blessed our family life.

After we reached Kerala, we celebrated our honeymoon in a beautiful hotel in Kanyakumari. Later, we visited interesting places like Kovalum, Ootty, and Vrindavanam in Mysore. We also visited all our families and friends in Kerala. As we were enjoying these days, we had to put a sudden break to it. Chinnamma's two months' leave was over, and she had to return to Doha to work. We both greatly suffered the separation that happened so soon. Especially for

Chinnamma, as a few days after arriving in Doha, she came to know she was pregnant. At that time, she very much desired my presence and company.

By the grace of God, I received my Qatar visa within two months. Chinnamma had made arrangements for it before going on leave. As soon as I got my visa, I resigned my job and made arrangements for my journey. With my special contacts and recommendations, I got my passport within one week. Thus, my twelve years of life in Bombay was coming to an end. I have many good memories to carry with me. Yearly Christmas, Diwali, and New Year celebrations, exhibitions, circuses, Navy Day celebrations, football plays, Juhu beach visits, friends, families, and coworkers. I bid farewell to all of them and boarded a flight on January 30, 1969. There was a stopover and a plane change in Bahrain. Finally, I reached Doha in a smaller plane and into the hands of Chinnamma.

CHAPTER 4

⚬⚭⚬

An Important Turning Point

When I reached Doha, I was surprised to see that country. It was a dry, barren desert. There was nothing modern or anything attractive there at that time. There were only a few buildings that were three to five story in height. Among the buildings were the Palace of the Ruler, a two-story hospital building, and the Oasis Hotel. There were some large and enclosed palaces of a few sheiks, the members of the ruling family, and a public place called Rayyan Garden. There were hardly any trees, birds, or greenery. Many of the one-story houses were made of mud and bamboo. They were good for the extreme hot climate. There were some two-story houses and shops that were of cement construction.

But one thing surprised me: Almost all Qataris, and even the male servants of the sheiks, drove big American cars. There were plenty of Mercedes-Benzes also. Doha, the capital of Qatar, was the only city, and it was only about five square miles. There were no buses or public transportation. But there were plenty of taxi cars available. The Arab women were all clad in purdah, and they were not allowed to drive or do office work. Their main job was bringing up their children. The lifestyle of the ruling family sheiks was quite different. They had big houses, lot of servants, and many cars; they had a busy life and spent much of the hot summer months in London or other cooler European countries.

In those days, the British government ruled Qatar and the nearby Gulf States. Also, there were a lot of British, Dutch, and Americans working in the oil companies. They all had modern accommodations and maintained Western lifestyles, and there were a few Western-style supermarkets and department stores to cater for them. There were two British banks and two or three Arab banks also.

Among the Indian community, nursing was the main job. They were all working in the two government hospitals. Their husbands also worked in other government departments, banks, shops, or small offices. Some people had good jobs in oil companies or at the airport. It was very difficult for newcomers to get good jobs.

The working hours in the government offices were from 7:00 a.m. to 2:00 p.m. But the private offices and the shops worked from 8:00 a.m. to noon and 4:00 p.m. to 8:00 p.m. because it was very hot in the midafternoon, and everybody took a nap for an hour or two. The beginning salary of an office worker in the private sector was 400 to 450 riyals (one riyal was worth two Indian rupees in those days). The cost of living was very low. Even gold was very cheap and plenty available in Doha. Many of the offices were air-conditioned. Some houses had air conditioners, but electricity was in short supply. Sometimes, the electricity went out, and it took two to three days to come back. In those days, Qatar didn't have enough electricity. On top of that, occasionally, we used to get shamals (hot air storms and sandstorms). When they came, everything and every place would be covered with dust. There was no greenery or natural beauty in Qatar at that time, and in the beginning, I often compared it with my beautiful state of Kerala and felt disappointed.

Many changes took place in the next few years, after it became independent in 1971 and before I left Doha for America in 1983. But I could not believe my eyes when I revisited Doha in 2002. The changes and progress Qatar made was impossible to believe. It had become one of the most beautiful places with spectacular high-rise buildings, beautiful gardens, modern roads and fountains, many hotels, and huge shopping malls. It was more than a hundred times progress. Then I realized that if you are an independent country with freedom and money, you can make a desert into a blooming place and transform a mud village into a modern metropolitan city. I witnessed it in Qatar. All other gulf countries have progressed like that. It was so difficult to find a job in early 1970s, but now hundreds of thousands of people are finding jobs there and making a good future for themselves.

I arrived in Doha in 1969, and for two or three months, I did not search for a job. Then I went out looking for a job. I visited the major department stores and checked for vacancies. As I had salesman experience, I preferred a salesman's job. On the second or third day, I got a job as a showroom salesman in a leading department store called Salam Studio and Stores. As I mentioned earlier, those stores catered mainly for the needs of European and American customers. As they found out that I was a smart fellow, after a few months, they gave me some more responsible office work. When I did that well, the manager appointed me an assistant in his office. I worked there for nearly a year.

In the meantime, we had our first baby girl, Jean. She was born in August, a very hot month. We had an air conditioner, but it was not cooling well. And sometimes, due to the overloads, there were power cuts, and it often stayed off for two or three days. The baby used to cry due to the intolerable heat. Then I had to take her to the terrace to get some cool air. I could only do this after sunset, otherwise the baby's skin would burn. Luckily, we had a concrete building with a terrace on it.

One year after joining Salam Studio, an opening for a court clerk became available in the office of the political agency (the office of the agent of the British government). One Mr. Wilson D'Souza, an Indian from Goa, was a counselor in the political agency. He informed our manager that they were looking for a reliable and smart person to fill the vacancy of a court clerk. My manager mentioned my name and asked me to apply for it. As far as I knew, it was very difficult to get a job in the political agency or in an oil company locally. Whenever they needed someone, they would recruit people from India and other countries through their recruiting agency, like BP India. They would interview many and select the highest qualified. Indians in Doha tried many times to get these good office jobs and failed.

Because I knew all these things, I did not bother to send the application. After a week, Mr. D'Souza called my manager and asked him what happened to his man. He said they had interviewed many and a decision would be made in a day or two. He also asked to send me personally the same day for an interview. My manager immediately asked me to go for the interview. I left the office, went home, put on my suit, and went to see Mr. D'Souza. He informed the political agent and was told that the interview will take place in one hour. I had no hope at all, but I went because I had been asked to go. I filled the application in Mr. D'Souza's office, and when I looked around and saw the office and staff, I wanted to work there and prayed to God to help me.

An hour later, the British secretary of the political agent came and took me to his office (a political agent is more powerful than an ambassador). When I entered, three people were waiting for me. They asked me to sit down and introduced themselves to me. One was Edward Henderson, the political agent; the second was Mr. Phillip Mansley, assistant political agent and head of chancery; the third was Mr. Douglas Hurd, commercial secretary, who was the head of the Commercial Section. This was the first time I had gone through such a high-level interview. But as I used to deal with many Europeans as a salesman, I could communicate well with them without fear. So, I depended on God, said a one-second prayer like Nehemiah, and answered all their questions boldly and correctly.

However, there were two shortcomings for me. First, I was the least qualified among those interviewed. Many were more qualified than me. But I was good at understanding and communicating in the English language. Second, because the local people and the police officers who brought cases spoke Arabic, the court clerk needed to know Arabic. The court clerk should be able to understand and answer them.

I could understand a few Arabic words and said that was not a big problem; I would learn Arabic soon. They asked me how, and I said I would hire an Arabic tutor. I think they understood my self-confidence and smartness. When the interview was over, they told me they had interviewed a number of graduates who knew Arabic and were residents of Doha for a long time. They also told me about the terms and conditions of the job. They informed me that whoever was selected had to go through three months of probation and the transfer of sponsorship. They also said they would let me know their decision later. As many more qualified people were interviewed, I didn't have much hope. But the salary and other benefits were very attractive, and I once again prayed to God to help me and went away.

To my surprise, they called me the next day and offered me the job; I could join them immediately. It was a miracle that I got a job so soon, with three times the salary I was getting in Salam Studio, with free accommodation and free medical coverage and passage to India for the whole family. I knew it was not because of my qualifications or smartness but because of the grace and blessings of God. I thanked God and made a commitment to give 10 percent of my salary for God's work. It happened by God, and it was a miracle in our eyes.

When I informed Salam Studio that I got a job in the British political agency, the proprietor didn't want to let me go. He said he found me to be smart and reliable. I told him that even if I worked with him for my whole life, he could not pay me what I was getting at the political agency, and he should not stand against a God-given opportunity. I prayed to God and begged the proprietor not to spoil my good future. As a result of my prayer, he agreed to release me. I was filled with happiness and thanked God for working in his mind. He was also a God-fearing person and a prominent businessman, who had good relationships with British business firms and the political agency.

The political agency had a British court in that building. A foreign national had worked as the court clerk for a very long time. Because he was caught in some serious wrongdoing, he was deported to his own country, and that was how this position became available. When I took the position in January 1970, I was instructed about the importance of faithfulness and truthfulness. It was indeed my strong determination to follow that policy in that job and throughout my life. Initially, I was taken on a two-year contract and on condition that if the court closed, the contract would not be renewed.

Even though I had no previous experience as a court clerk, I committed everything in the hands of God and started the work. Though there was a court in Doha, there was no sitting or resident judge there. There were several judges and a chief judge based in Bahrain to cover Abu Dhabi, Dubai, Sharjah, Bahrain, Kuwait, Oman, and Qatar. According to the number of cases filed and its need, on request from each country, the judges visited them and remained there until all cases are finished. For serious criminal cases and appeal cases, the chief judge would come. The assistant political agent acted as the court registrar.

After taking up the job, I understood the importance and responsibility of the position. I had to register civilian cases, collect the court fees, keep the accounts, undertake insolvency cases and take control of stock and finance of the insolvent company, protect the company's property with the help of the police, dispose of goods and properties through auction, settle between parties certain unmerited civil matters, register criminal cases such as fighting and murder that are brought by the police, send the accused criminals to jail, and post cases for hearing after agreeing with prosecutors, plaintiffs, defendants and their lawyers, and the judge.

I realized that I had a very important and responsible job to perform. As the court clerk, if I called any police officer, the commandant of police, or a military officer, they would immediately appear in the court and salute me. Once, I visited the prison along with the registrar to assess the welfare of the prisoners. I was surprised at the high respect the registrar and I received. Within a few months, almost everyone in the city, from the merchants to the police officers, knew me. I used to get high respect wherever I went in the city. But I never misused the power and position I had.

One year after I joined the political agency, the British government gave independence to all the Gulf States. So, in 1971, the political agency became the British Embassy, and the political agent, H. E. Edward Henderson, became the first ambassador to Qatar. With that change, all the British courts in the Gulf States were closed, and local courts were established.

During the next few months, I closed all the case files, recorded everything, and sent it to London. There were also some unfinished cases that had to be handed over to the local courts. Even after finishing my court work, there were some more months to finish my contract. During that period, I was given the opportunity to fill in and assist leave vacancies in the Counselor and Commercial departments. I did all that very well and happily. Before Judge Miller left Qatar, he gave me a certificate stating that he was very pleased with my work as a court clerk.

One month after joining the political agency, we moved to a large villa nearby. I agreed to give more rent than the owner asked, because the house allowance I received was more than the owner asked. That house belonged to the driver and personal bodyguard of the ruler of Qatar, Sheikh Hamad bin Khalifa Al Thani. When a new palace was built in Rayyan, the ruler moved to Rayyan, and his bodyguard also moved.

The house that I moved into was a large one, with many bedrooms, a large kitchen and wide veranda, a large concrete courtyard, and a garage. It had an eight-foot-high boundary wall and a huge iron gate. Because the courtyard was very big, we turned it into a shuttlecock court. Even some of my friends parked their expensive cars in my courtyard when they went on long leave to India.

With the help of the embassy, we brought a servant girl from Kerala, and we had a comfortable good life. My office hours were 7:30 a.m. to 1:00 p.m. My office was less than five minutes from my home. Once my work was over, I used to pick up Chinnamma from Rumela Government Hospital, which was located just behind our embassy building. So, by 1:15, she and I would be back in our home from work. After eating lunch served by the girl, we switched on the air conditioner and went to sleep. By about four o'clock, the servant would wake us up, saying tea was ready. Once that was over, our friends would come and have a social get-together. The ladies continued with their talk, and we men went to the court and played shuttlecock. We even installed floodlights to play at night. Sometimes, we played drafts or chess. On Sunday evenings, we had our worship meetings, and once a week, we had our church prayer meetings.

I used to get all the British holidays and local holidays. Additionally, every now and then, we used to have big cocktail parties in the embassy for occasions like the Queen's birthday, royal visits, trade mission visits, and new postings and departures of diplomats. It was compulsory for me to attend, sometimes Chinnamma came as well. Once I had arranged a party in our house. The British ambassador and many of the embassy staff attended. In addition, the Indian chargé d'affaires and a few other diplomats from other embassies also attended.

Thus, we were having a very happy life there. I remember some of my close friends telling me they felt jealous of me. In all that time, I realized that it was not because of my ability or greatness, but it was of the grace and kindness of God. And I thanked and praised my God for it. In between, we were blessed with our second daughter; Judy was born in December 1970. Thus, our happiness was at the top.

When my two-year contract was over, they renewed it for another two years. I was a little concerned as to what would happen to me, as the court had been closed. But because they were very impressed with my work and satisfied with my ability to take on any kind of job, with the help of God, they decided to retain me for two more years. But it was a small embassy, and there were no openings that could accommodate me. Therefore, they promoted a person in the Commercial Department and placed me in his position. I was given the job of commercial archivist. I worked in that position for two years. Before my term was over, the head of the Commercial Department contacted the Foreign and Commonwealth Office in London and obtained permission to renew my contract. With the renewal of the contract, I was also promoted to commercial assistant. The next two years, I worked as a commercial assistant to the full satisfaction of everyone.

In between this, an interesting event occurred. When I was promoted to commercial assistant, a lady took over from me as commercial archivist. She came in with some influence and recommendations. She was the wife of an official in a ministry in the Qatar government. After a few months, this influential and cunning lady planned to kick me out and take my position. So, she complained to my boss that I misbehaved with her. When my boss called me and advised me that I should behave decently with coworkers, I was taken aback. I did not know what he meant, as I have never misbehaved with anyone. Confused, I said OKAY and went back to my office.

But my loving God doesn't like innocent men like me to be harmed. He knew that if she remained there, I would be in trouble. So, to save me, He passed the judgment against her. She continued with her crooked ideas, and one day, she passed on some confidential information to her husband working in the local government, and on another occasion, she called and tried to speak directly with his boss, a sheikh, and a minister. The annoyed minister called our ambassador and complained about her bad behavior. Within half an hour, our section head called me in and asked me to take the key from her and make sure she did not touch anything official. Thus, she was gone.

After independence, suddenly, there was new life and energy in the industrial, manufacturing, and commercial areas of the country. Small shopkeepers and members of the ruling families and other prominent Qataris all started new businesses, offices, and retail shops. Hundreds of people from foreign governments, manufacturers, distributors, consultants, and contractors, mainly from Europe and the United States, started pouring into Qatar and other Gulf States. But many of them didn't know the culture and the language of the Arab countries. Therefore, the first contact point for the British businessmen was the Commercial Department in the British Embassy, Doha, Qatar.

Some businessmen would come alone with direct contact to us. Some would come through the British government's Department of Trade and Industry, and some would come as a group in a trade mission under the sponsorship of a local Chamber of Commerce in the UK. All of them would write to us months in advance, giving the details of their products and services with booklets and literature. They would also let us know the purpose of their visit and what kind of assistance they needed from us. The commercial secretary and officers would find out the suitable contacts from the local government departments and business community. Sometimes, we would recommend local agency representation and produce a status report of the recommended company. We prepared all this information and sent it to them or kept it ready for their arrival.

When they arrived in Doha, they'd come and see the officers they corresponded with.

Commercial officers had their own big separate offices. When businessmen arrived at the reception, our British secretary informed us, brought them to our office, and arranged coffee or tea for us. These interviews usually lasted half an hour. We would hand over the file containing the contacts, recommendations, and status reports. They would be very pleased and thankful. Many times, after they returned to UK, they would write back to us about the contracts or business they made and their success stories. It used to give me tremendous joy to see this. Sometimes, the visitors would be managing directors of a large company or industry official, under whom hundreds or even thousands of people may be working. When such high officials came and sat in front of this matriculate and took advice from me and expressed their gratitude, you know how proud and satisfied I felt.

In those days, when a British trade mission came, the commercial secretary and commercial officers would go and receive them at the airport. Because of the respect and influence the UK government had among the Qataris at that time, we could go up to the tarmac near the aircraft and receive them. Then they were brought out through the VIP area. We often briefed them in the VIP lounge itself and handed over the contacts list and briefing files. Then we would drive them in our own cars to the hotels. Our embassy driver would take their luggage in the Land Rover and bring it to the hotel. Usually on the same evening, we would have a large reception arranged at the ambassador's residence, which was adjacent to the embassy building. Ambassador would invite the heads of government departments, high industry officials, consultants, contractors, bank managers, oil company officials, and so on. It was our responsibility to introduce them to the mission visitors. We used to get high appreciation and respect at those moments.

The same way, every year, the ambassador used to celebrate the Queen's birthday with a big party. At that time, important government officials, businessmen, leaders in the society, ambassadors of all diplomatic missions, and other prominent people were invited. I had the opportunity to meet and maintain friendly relationships with many of them. I continued enjoying this wonderful job until 1983. How many visitors? How many parties? How many changing ambassadors and other officials? The diplomats had to go back every three years. Those were very happy and enjoyable days.

Chinnamma and I visited London many times during this period. By this time, we had one more daughter born. But she had heart problems at birth and was taken to London for open-heart surgery, but she did not survive. In this connection, we were in London for a few days, and she was buried in London.

In 1974, when we went on our annual leave to India, I was able to buy some land in a prominent place in Ranny town, and my father began to construct a modern two-story house there. That was completed in 1976. On our second visit to India, my mom and dad and I moved to this house. From then until the year 2000, this spacious house was used to accommodate visiting speakers of conventions, travelling evangelists, and many others. I am glad to say that this house was used as a resting place for many needy ones. In those days, people in Doha and other Gulf States used to send their money back to India via Hundi (an unofficial way). But as a matter of principle and as a child of God, I sent all my money through proper bank transfers. Though I got a lower rate, I was not a loser because God provided me a beautiful piece of land at a very reasonable price. Also, the house was built without any cheating by the contractor. Not only that, because of my honesty, the good Lord saved me from the net some jealousy people had spread for me. They had complained to the Revenue Department that all my money was black money, but when I showed them the actual transfer records, they cancelled the case on the spot and appreciated my honesty. I thank God for saving me from my enemies.

Within the next few years, Rev. Dr. Matthew Adackapara, Chinnamma's elder brother, asked us to join him in America, where he now lived. But because we both had very good jobs and a happy life in Doha, we said no. I had some other cousins also living in the US. Therefore, I had a slight inclination in my mind that one day, we should move there. When I mentioned this idea to my parents, they were against it. The reason for their objection was the distance.

At that time, it took many days to come from the US, even in an emergency. As I was their only son, they didn't want me to be far away from them.

In 1979, Chinnamma's younger brother, Scaria Adackapara moved with his family to the United States. After they arrived, they compelled us to move there too. Though we had no plans to immigrate, we decided to visit America and see the place and our people there. So, we arranged a two-month tour, including Rome, Paris, London, New York, and Washington. Accordingly, after spending nearly two weeks in Rome, Paris, and London, we reached New York and then New Jersey, where my brother-in-law was staying.

In the next month and a half, we visited many places in New York, New Jersey, Washington, Philadelphia, and Connecticut. We also visited many of our friends, families, and relatives. Many of them had their own houses, and their parents and siblings stayed with them or nearby. I was very much impressed by their living standards and the modern style of the cities and the country itself. Whereas Doha was still underdeveloped, and we couldn't own a house or remain there permanently. Once our job ended, we had to leave the country. Not only that, but we also cannot have our parents or other dear ones with us on long-term basis. Even our two daughters were in boarding school in India. When we realized that we could live together with our children, own a house, work, and even become US citizens, our mind and attitude towards America changed, and we asked our brother-in-law to file our application for immigration.

Within two years of filing the application, our visa was approved. After Chinnamma and I came to the United States to obtain our green cards, we went back to Doha and resigned our jobs. Because I was a permanent contract staff, I had to give three months' notice. I submitted my resignation on March 1. The ambassador and all other staff liked me and were very satisfied with my work, so they were unwilling to release me. Because of my insistence, they finally agreed and accepted my resignation. I worked there in the embassy for twelve years. When I remember those days, I have nothing but sweet memories. It was a real blessing to work in the Foreign Services

Department of the British government with the well-cultured and well-behaved diplomats as a family, without any discrimination of race, color, or nationality. I was given equal opportunity and the respect I deserved. They sent me to a larger British embassy in Kuwait and to the Department of Trade and Industry in London for training. By giving me promotions and opportunities, they helped me to grow. When I remember those British officials, my heart is filled with gratitude and thanksgiving. If I was working in an Indian embassy or another Indian organization, I would have never attained these positions. Our own people might have worked against me and kicked me out on account of my educational qualifications.

Once in every week, the ambassador used to have a meeting in his office with the commercial counselor and the commercial officers. At that time, he used to announce our individual achievements, discuss future plans, and inquire about our personal opinions. I had equal voice and consideration like others in the meeting. I remember I had received some appreciation letters from cabinet ministers in London. During my work there, HH Queen Elizabeth and her husband Prince Phillip made a state visit to Qatar to meet Sheikh Khalifa bin Hammed Al Thani. After the official visit, the Queen and Prince visited the British Embassy. Along with other embassy staff members, Chinnamma and I were given the opportunity to meet Queen Elizabeth and Prince Phillip and shake hands with them. It is also noteworthy that I too was given an independent office room like other British officers and the service of a British secretary. Indeed, it was a matter of great pride for me to have that position and status in Doha at that time. Once again, I confess that it was all because of the grace of God.

With the intention of getting me a job in New York, our ambassador, Sir Stephen Day, gave me a very good service certificate and a letter of recommendation to the management counselor in the British Consulate in New York. He also gave a letter of introduction to the personnel manager in the United Nations, whom he knew when he worked there earlier as a member of the UK mission to the United Nations. In addition, before my departure from Doha, the ambassador arranged a large farewell party for me and Chinnamma.

Like trade mission parties, a few government officials, bank managers, businessmen, and staff members and their partners were invited. After a short speech from the ambassador and giving me a valuable gift, the embassy staff bid farewell to me. I am always grateful to the ambassador and the other diplomatic staff for the love and support they showered upon me. I cannot forget the love and regard shown for me by the non-diplomatic permanent staff, like Wilson D'Souza, Mohammed Hussein, Sabri Thawabi, P. S. Nair, Vernie D'Souza, Sifat Gul, Mahamood, Ahmed, and Antony.

It was more heartbreaking and painful for us to leave our friends and family members. One of my sisters, three brothers-in-law, two nieces, two nephews, and some cousins from my side lived in Doha, and so did Chinnamma's sister's son and daughter. They were P. V. Mathai, Sunny Matthew, Raju and Kunjumol, and their children, Babukutty, Kunjumole and Kunjumon and their children, Lizy, Thampi and their children; Joy and Elsy; Joy; and Mary. We were the reason for many of them to come to Doha. And almost all of them stayed with us for some period of time. Therefore, they all loved us very much. Even my father and mother had the privilege to come and stay with us for a few months. Those were all wonderful times in our life.

We also had a good number of close friends in Doha. They all advised us not to leave the very good job and benefits we had. They said it was madness to do so. In fact, we lost a lot of money by making this decision. But the greatest consolation and benefit was that our children would be with us, and they would grow up in our presence, with our love and care.

When we take the Malayalee community of Doha, in those days, except for one or two senior staff in the oil companies, I had the best-paid and most-respected job and position. I am not saying this to show pride but to let others know how God can bless His children who love Him. I mentioned earlier about my office and position. Additionally, commercial officers could take appointments and see any heads of government departments and managers and proprietors of major business organizations. We could even obtain company secrets like capital, turnover, profits and loss, and other details to prepare status reports of the companies. We used this information to recommend them for agencies to British products and services. Because of this, the managers and proprietors liked us very much, as we could give them much more profits. Our office hours were 7:30 a.m. to 1:00 p.m., which was less than the local government or oil companies' timings. We were provided with furnished modern accommodations, full medical coverage for the whole family, more local holidays, and thirty days' leave every year. Once in every two years, we got full family passage back to India. In addition to airfare, we could also claim the taxi fare and porterage. I had a big American car and another Japanese car. It was all by the grace of God, because there were more qualified people than me, and without the help of God, I could not have achieved it. Many people would hesitate to leave such permanent job and take a risk. But I was confident that my good Lord would provide me all my needs, as he promised, wherever I may be.

Among our close friends, Kunjunju and Thankamma family, Rajan and Achamma family, Kunjmon and Lilly family, Kunju and Annamma family, George and Mercy family, Joy and Molly family, Podikunju and Chinnamma family, and Felix D'Souza and Jessica family are impossible to forget.

The love our church members had for us and their grief in our leaving is impossible to explain. I was a founding member of the Ebenezer Brethren Assembly and very much a part and parcel of every activity there. The church initially gathered in our house for a few years, and even the address was in care of me. Our family was there in the forefront of every need and action. The commendation letter, gifts, and silver plaque that were given to us by the church is evidence of their affection.

Before we left for America, we held a farewell get-together in our house. My friends, family, relatives, and church members were invited. We can never forget the farewell kisses, hugs, and tears. Church members like Thankachen and Gracy, Babu and Baby, Joy and Thankamma, Aniyankunju and Ammal, Jose and Thankamma, and Charly were especially close and dear to us.

Finally, on June 30, 1983, we left Doha as a family and started our journey towards America. On the way, we stayed in London for two days, and on July 2, 1983, we reached New York. Chinnamma's younger brother Appachan and some of his friends met us at the airport and took us to his residence in Elizabeth, New Jersey. Appachan, Leelamma and his family, and Chinnamma's elder brother, Rev. Dr. Matthew Adackapara, were all very happy that we had come to the United States. From that day onwards, Appachan's friends Jose and Valsamma, Benny and Ammini, and Georgekutty and Omana became our friends also.

My mind was still wandering through the memories of the past several years. By this time, the Russian foreign minister had finished his speech, and someone else took his place. As the day session was coming to an end, I also put a stop to my thoughts, left behind my memories, and walked out of the UN Assembly Hall.

Once again, after a long period of time, I had the opportunity to dig through my mind and recollect the memories and experiences I had since arriving in America. I was on my way to India on a flight from New York. I was on a fourteen-hour journey, and the time was moving very slowly.

After a sumptuous dinner, many people pulled the blankets over them and went to sleep. Others were very much awake and watching their favorite programs on their own television screens. But I was not engaged in either of these activities. My mind was feeding me a picture of two decades of time that had passed since we arrived in the States, until my retirement from my job in 2000.

CHAPTER 5

———⊶⊷———

The Call of the Magic World

After coming to America, I spent the first three weeks taking care of some official matters, like registering with the Social Security Agency, enrolling both my daughters in nearby schools, and obtaining driving licenses for me and Chinnamma. (In those days, if you had a driving license from the Middle East, you only needed to pass a written test to get a US license.) And visiting immediate family members and friends was on my list of initial tasks.

Once that was completed, my attention turned to finding a job. I learned from family and friends that getting a job at that time was very difficult. I was told that many highly qualified and experienced people from India had come and remained without a job for months, and afterwards got a job in some factory or gas station. That information disappointed me. In those days, the economic situation was very bad, and the unemployment rate was very high. The opportunities in the private sectors were very rare.

Therefore, I decided to go and see someone in the British Consulate in Midtown New York. I went there and saw the management officer and handed him the recommendation letter the ambassador in Doha had given me. I also gave my local address and telephone number and requested that I be informed if any commercial officer vacancies arise. He told me a vacancy for a commercial officer's position hardly ever occurs, and even if one became available, it would be given to a local American citizen with the knowledge and experience of local markets and business laws. He asked me if I wanted to be informed of any other openings that arose, and I said that I did.

For newcomers in the US, even if they are well qualified in their own countries, they have to study more in the US and pass many examinations, tests, and interviews to get a good job in a good office. For a moment, I felt bad for leaving the good job in Doha and coming here. Then I put my trust in the good Lord and prayed to Him to open up a new way for me. Let me say that the good Lord heard my prayer. Within two weeks, I received a telephone call from the British Consulate. I was told there was an opening for an accounts clerk in the Accounts Department, and if I was interested, I should go and see them. Even though accounting was not my line, I thought, *let me go and find out the details and salary scale.* So I went and saw the administrative officer. Because I was an ex British embassy staff, he treated me like a friend and gave me details of the work involved, grade, and the salary. I was shocked when I heard it. In New York, they don't take any contract staff, as there are plenty of British, Irish, and Americans available to fill the positions. All were local appointments. The salary was half of what I was getting in Doha, a grade lower, and no accommodation or travel allowances. Medical coverage and pension were there. And it was far better than what the private sector offered in those days. So I thought for a while, prayed to God in my mind, and decided not to refuse the first offer I got in USA.

I agreed to accept the position and was asked to start the coming Monday. When I thought about it on my way back home, I realized that it was the grace of God that I got a job within a month of my arrival in the US, in a beautiful midtown office, without any further studies, application, tests, or interviews. I thanked God for His provision. When I reached home and told my people, they said it was good that I accepted it. With that, one of my wishes was also being accomplished. When we came on a visit to New York three years ago, I was so impressed with the high-rise buildings in Manhattan and wished in my mind that if God permits, I should get a job in one of those buildings. I thanked God for fulfilling my wish.

But the case was different for Chinnamma. Though she was a registered nurse in India and Doha, her those qualifications were not enough to become an RN here. She had to go through many procedures. First of all, she had to pass the GED exam (high school equivalency), pass a TOEFL exam, study psychiatry, and then pass an LPN exam, and then pass the state board examination. These were very difficult procedures for nurses coming from India, especially in their late forties and early fifties. Many had taken many years to cross this bar, and some failed to reach their goal. But because Chinnamma was a hard-working and dedicated person, she became an RN in less than five years.

As my brother-in-law and his family were Catholics, they used to go to a nearby Catholic church. We were of Brethren and Protestant beliefs and therefore sought out a Brethren Assembly to worship. When we inquired, we came to know that there was one in the Bronx and one in Little Neck, Long Island, both in New York. It was very time consuming and tedious to reach these assemblies from where we were staying in New Jersey. However, the word went around and reached Brother George Abraham, who was a UN employee residing in Staten Island. He was originally from my own town in Ranny, Kerala. He was a member of the India Gospel Assembly, gathering in Little Neck. Brother Abraham contacted me and offered to come and pick us up and take us to church. It was a tough task. He had to cross the Goethals Bridge, pay tolls, and travel to our home. We agreed, and for a few weeks, he used to pick us up and take us to church and bring us back home. It was at least a fifty-mile one-way journey. On top of that, he used to pick up another old couple from Staten Island. Luckily, he had a large station wagon and could accommodate all of us, in addition to his own family. I was impressed at his sacrificial mind to do it in the love of God.

As two months passed by, I was very concerned about Brother George Abraham's hard work. I borrowed my brother-in-law's car and started driving around to familiarize myself with the American roads and traffic rules. I found it very easy, as we in Doha also had left-hand driving. So, I decided to buy a car. Usually, a newcomer in those days would start with a second-hand car and pay off the loan in three to four years' time. But I went to a car dealer and bought a brand-new Oldsmobile Cutlass Supreme, a big car, paying the full price in cash. It was a surprise for the car dealer and many of our people. This was three months after we arrived in the US. From next Sunday onwards, I drove to church and back myself. I will never forget the help Brother Abraham rendered to us when we had no vehicle of our own.

Once we started coming to the church by our own means, many people in the church, especially close friends like Baby Mathew and Elsy, Thampi and Alice, Monachen and Ammini urged us to move to New York, near the church. After Brother Baby Mathew bought a house in Elmont, they pressed hard, and we decided to move to New York. We looked at many houses in and around Elmont and Bellerose and finally decided on one in Elmont, very conveniently located, close to the highway.

As I mentioned about the car, in case of the house, it was the same. Newcomers usually will stay in an apartment or in a basement apartment with someone else for five to ten years and then buy a house, paying ten to twenty thousand dollars down payment and the balance in a twenty- or thirty-year mortgage. We the Indians are very prestigious and that is why by hard work or double work we will earn and save some money and buy a house as early as possible, because we want to look good in front of others. There are many other people, who come from different parts of the world and even the locals, who stay in apartments throughout their life. They spend what they make and live happily.

In those days, people coming from India could bring only eight dollars per person. That is one reason they had to stay in an apartment and work hard. If we were coming from India, our condition would have been the same. But by the grace of God, we could bring more than $125,000 cash from Doha. It was a big amount in 1983. We were also able to bring a number of household appliances and electronic equipment from Doha. At that time, many wise and experienced people asked me to invest in one or two houses or some other stock investments. If I had done that, I would probably have millions now. But as I came from Doha and had never borrowed anything in the past, I thought it would be a shame to be a debtor to anyone.

So, I bought a house, putting a down payment of eighty-five thousand dollars and purchasing new furniture and equipment worth another twenty-five thousand dollars against cash payment. So, on January 15, 1984, six months after arriving in the US, we moved into our own house in New York. Though I was renting a much larger villa in Doha, I felt good and happy that I could be an owner of a house in New York. I knew it was all because of the grace of God, and I thanked him for that.

I do not consider it a loss or a mistake to have paid that much cash up front for the house, car, and furniture. Because of that, I had a very nominal mortgage payment to make every month. We could easily pay that with our salary. Therefore, Chinnamma never had to work double duty or night shift. Debt was never a burden for us. We could easily pay all our bills and credit card invoices every month, without paying any interest or penalty. I am not saying all this to show pride. But my good Lord was graceful to provide me with more than I asked. This is my testimony on God's provision and goodness to me.

Another positive thing was that we both were always at home in the evenings. Therefore, we could have our daily evening prayer with the children and bring them up in the knowledge and fear of God. It was a great advantage, and therefore, we had no problem or worries about the children. I am saying all these things for the glory of God, because I am aware of many parents who suffered a lot because of their children, as they were not there with them when needed.

CHAPTER 6

The Abundance of God's Grace

Within a few days of joining the office, I learned all the work very easily and did it well. The accountant, Mr. Tom Booker, was very pleased with my work and started giving me more responsibilities. As he found me faithful, he also gave me the responsibility of handling cash and other banking. Every day, we had to deposit the consular fee collection and withdraw from the bank ten, twenty, and sometimes fifty thousand dollars, as required. Sometimes, when the UN delegation and other ministerial visits occurred, I had to draw up to one hundred thousand dollars in cash. Even though the bank was nearby, we had to go and come in an official car. There was a British driver and a British security officer for every bank trip.

One day, a frightening thing happened. I was at the bank counter along with the security officer, depositing our money. Suddenly, we heard a gunshot and confusion. When we looked back, we saw two huge people standing there, pointing rifles at the customers and staff. They shouted that no one should move, and everyone should stand with their hands raised up. We all did that. A third person came to the counters and gave each cashier a cloth bag and told them to fill it up with cash.

All the cashiers did as they were told. When the robbers got the money, they fired one more shot at the ceiling and ran away. When I looked at my British security officer, I saw he was all pale and sweating. He was much older than me and had high blood pressure. No one can blame him. I had trusted in God and stood there without any movement or fear. By the grace of God, nothing untoward happened. The robbers escaped with hundreds of thousands of dollars. Usually when they do this sort of bank robbery, they shoot someone, so nobody follows them. I thank God for protecting us from death or any other mishap.

In New York, the British Foreign and Commonwealth Office had many offices. They are the UK mission to the UN, headed by an ambassador and a deputy ambassador. Then there was the British Consulate, headed by a consul general. There were British Trade Offices and British Information Services. Altogether, there were more than two hundred people working in these offices; about seventy-five were diplomats deputed from London, and the rest were local staff. Of all the staff, 90 percent were British and 10 percent American nationals. I was the only Indian national.

The Management Department was taking care of all these people's matters, and also of the visitors and delegates, including ministerial and royal visits. I was one of the management staff. Every three years, we had a staff inspection. The inspectors would come from London and stay for a few weeks, going through all the performance reports and interviewing each and every staff member. Then they'd decide whether that position was to be retained or cancelled, or if someone was to be promoted or so on. Luckily, this Indian was one of only two or three persons promoted during that year's inspection. I was promoted to assistant accountant, from the accounts clerk's position. I felt really proud and happy, and thanked God for His grace and blessing.

Diplomats and all other staff in the Foreign Services had to keep a high standard of living and code of conduct. That was the rule. Nobody would ever utter a bad word in public or in the office. Everybody would come to work wearing a full suit, throughout the year. For thirty years, throughout my service with the British Embassy, I used to wear suit every day. In New York, we all had a pass to enter the UN building anytime. Many times, at lunchtime, I used to have lunch (alone or with friends) at the huge UN staff canteen. There were also occasions when our management counselor and other diplomats would take us for lunch to the delegates' exclusive and beautiful restaurant. Moreover, we had a party almost every week in our office. Ministerial visits, delegate visits, diplomats arriving on new postings and departing, and so on. There may be a hundred reasons to conduct a cocktail party.

In addition, once in a while, our heads of departments would take all the members of that department to the best restaurants in Manhattan for lunch. These lunch sessions would last two to three hours. At the time of Christmas and UN Assembly, the ambassador and the consul general would arrange big dinner parties at their residences for the staff and UN delegates. For those parties, Chinnamma and I were treated like royalty, like all others. I remember at one Christmas party in the British consul general's house, I had the privilege to dance with the consul general's wife. Many a time, I marveled at the equal treatment of ministers to the lowest grade employees in these parties. Those were the best example of employer-employee relations, which I could not see anywhere else. Those are great memories for a simple and humble person like me. But it all happened to me by the grace of God.

Initially, my parents in Kerala did not like my moving to the US. Their main concern was that their only son would be very far away from them. If anything happened to them, from Doha, we could reach Kerala in a few hours, whereas in their view, it would take days to get there from the US. Considering their concern, I planned to bring them to America on a visit and show them this was not so, to remove their worries about the distance. So even before I left Doha, I made arrangements for their visit to US. When I went to the American Embassy in Doha to collect our US immigrant visas, I told the consular officer there about my parents. I told him it was normally difficult for my parents to get a visiting visa for the US. So I asked him to issue a letter addressed to the consular officer in the American Consulate in Madras, India. As I was a British Embassy officer, and he an American Embassy officer, we considered ourselves coworkers. That was how he treated me. Not only that, but he also knew that in the near future, I would become an American citizen. That is why I took the courage to make such an unusual request. Let me say, by the grace of God, he immediately typed a letter to the visa-issuing officer in Madras, signed it, and gave it to me. In that letter, he wrote that V. J. Mathews is a person dear to him and his parents should be issued with a visiting visa. When this letter was shown to the counselor officer in Madras, visiting visas were issued to my parents without any questions asked. Therefore, I could bring them to the US within one year of our arrival here.

My parents came and stayed with us for three months. Within that period, we took them around to many places of interest in New York, New Jersey, Washington, and Toronto in Canada. Then they found out that the distance and traveling were not big problems. They especially liked these modern cities and the luxurious life we had. So, their worries about us being too far was gone, and they were happy that we moved to the US. We have many cousins and relatives here, and they were happy to visit and see them all. That year, the Summer Olympics were held in Atlanta. My father watched it throughout the day and enjoyed it very much. He was a sport enthusiast and played volleyball himself.

We were very happy that both our daughters, Jean and Judy, could be brought from the convent school in India; we enrolled them in a school near our home. In addition to my cousins, Chinnamma also had a number of family members here. More than that, we were able to make a large circle of friends within a short period of time. We also had good relations and fellowship with all our Malayali church community here. Thus, by the grace of God, we started enjoying life here also.

But I was upset in one matter, and it grieved my heart. When I looked through the Kerala Mission Fund (KEM) list for the past two or three years, I noticed that hardly anyone in the United States was contributing for God's work in India. There were three or four people giving four or five hundred rupees in a year from all over America. (I am not blaming anybody; maybe they were using some other source, but it was very rare in those days.) There was not a single name from New York in the list.

Grieved by this situation, I asked many believers why nobody was giving any money for Gospel work in India. The answer I got from all of them was that they were all big debtors and they had to repay their loans every month. They would buy houses worth hundreds of thousands of dollars, and buy new expensive cars, and live in luxury. But they couldn't give to God's work after finishing their loans.

I thought this was a wrong practice and decided to change that way of thinking. I decided to be an example, and in 1983, the year we immigrated to the US, I sent the KEM Fund twelve thousand rupees, as I used to do even when in Doha. In the following years, I kept increasing the amount and praying that God should work in the hearts of believers here. God answered my prayers, and the people acted upon it. If we look at the KEM Fund list for the following years, you can see a real difference. The spirit of giving spread among the believers all over the US, and from then onward, a lot of blessed work has been done by Brethren believers in the US, and still going on for the glory of God. I praise God for that.

After coming to America, my official life was very enjoyable and satisfying. I came across many people who came from Kerala with very high educational qualifications and experience, but they lived in disappointment and worries, without a decent job, proper position, or approval. Whereas an undeserving and unqualified person like me was lifted up, honored, and provided with a very decent job, by the grace of God. It may encourage readers to know how wonderfully and miraculously God worked to help a believer like me in my official level.

I want to highlight one or two examples in which I experienced abundant grace from God. I mentioned earlier that I was promoted to assistant accountant from the post of accounts clerk. After a few years, an impossible desire came into my mind that one day I should become the accountant. And I knew that there is nothing impossible with God, and that He will fulfill the desires of His loved ones. I myself am an example to prove that promise of God.

New York is one of the largest posts in the world (British embassies and consular offices in foreign countries are called "posts" by the British Foreign Services). Paris, Moscow, Islamabad, New Delhi, and Washington are among the largest posts. As the prime minister and foreign ministers used to attend the UN General Assembly almost every year, New York was also a very important and large post. The post was established more than a hundred years ago, and since then, the accountant position was held by a British diplomat from London. That was the rule with all the larger posts all over the world.

That was the position this unqualified, locally engaged Indian citizen desired. But as a miracle, either as an answer to my prayer or for the glory of God, that written rule was changed. The Treasury Department in London declared that henceforth, even larger posts could appoint locally engaged staff as accountants. When I heard this news, I rejoiced and thanked God for opening a way for me. When the three-year term for the London-based accountant was over, he went back, and no replacement was sent from the UK. So the vacancy was announced, and many people applied for it, including me. But I did not get that job. As ours was a computerized account, and someone with more computer experience was selected.

At first, I felt bad and disappointed as God opened a way, but my desire was not fulfilled. But later, I realized that God had done it for my goodness, because He knows everything in advance. In fact, God knew that if this very responsible position came to me without any previous experience, it was possible that I wouldn't be able to carry it for too long. God promised the land of Canaan to Abraham and the Israelites, but He handed it over to them after many years, when they had enough manpower to occupy and rule it. That was what God did to me in this case.

The new accountant was a very nice person. Within a period of one year, she taught me much about the accountant's job. She also allowed me to perform certain tasks that were her responsibility. I completed them all correctly and to her satisfaction. In addition, realizing my interest and enthusiasm in the new system, the management sent me to our embassy in Washington for training and to the diplomatic staff training center In London for additional training. All that helped me a lot with my work.

After one year, the accountant Janice Knight moved to Geneva to join her boyfriend. So another vacancy arose for the accountant's position. British chartered accountants (CAs) and Americans holding CPA degrees applied. Altogether there were seven applicants, including me. My qualifications were God's grace and His promise.

Two of the applicants were noteworthy. One was a British lady who was a CA residing in New York, whose husband was a private bank officer. The other one was a girl working in our own Accounts section. She was also British and hailing from the same place in the UK from where our management officer also came. They were close friends, as they were from the same place, and he had a special regard for her. I came to know about this through other staff members. The management officer was on the interviewing team. He also had an important and decisive say in the selection of the accountant, as he is the immediate boss to the accountant, and they should have a very good relationship between them, for the smooth an efficient running of the department.

Circumstances were against me, as I was an Indian without proper qualifications, and no help from anybody, but I committed everything to my good Lord and asked for His help. The date of the interview was given to us, a week in advance. All were to be interviewed on the same day, starting from 9:30, by a panel of four people, consisting of the management counselor, the management officer, the deputy ambassador, and the current accountant. They were the interviewing officers. Three days before the day of the interview, the management officer received a message that his mother-in-law was seriously sick and admitted in a hospital in New Zealand. So he and his wife left the next day for New Zealand. He was replaced for the interviews by the head of the British Information Services.

I thought it was the work of God answering to my prayers. There was no doubt it was so. With this event, I got more confident and believed that my God would work a miracle and help me. The day of the interviews came, and they were all over by one o'clock. We were told we'd be informed of their decision later. I went back to my office and continued with my work prayerfully. At about four o'clock, the management counselor came into my office and said I had been selected as the accountant. He shook my hand, congratulated me, and wished me good luck. I cannot explain the happiness and gratitude I had for God. My God is a God of miracles, and He does everything good for His children. All this happened by the grace of God.

This was a very important and respectful appointment. This position involved contacts and dealings with British embassies and consulates all over the world and even to the prime minister's office. The accountant was also the head of the Accounts section. It was a miracle for an Indian matriculate to get such a position in the British Foreign Services Department, brushing aside more qualified British and American nationals. The staff members in our New York office were very impressed by my achievement. How great and sweet is the grace and provision of God. Once again, I could taste and see that the Lord is good.

An interesting thing that happened is that the British chartered accountant who interviewed for the post of accountant accepted the assistant accountant's position that became available upon my promotion to accountant. She worked under me for two years and went back to the UK when her husband was transferred there. I was so surprised and impressed at this highly qualified British lady, who worked under an under-qualified Indian, so happily, faithfully, and humbly. During those two years, she never looked at me with anger or envy. She was always very humble, cooperative, and friendly.

In the same way, though the other girl the management officer was interested in did not get the job, he never behaved angrily or treated me badly. I would call it as the quality of their culture. Is it possible for Indians to behave like that? How cheap and mean are we Indians, including believers; we create problems, make accusations, argue, and even fight for the sake of name and position. For the next five years, I was the accountant and head of the Accounts Department. During that period, all the staff members who worked under me, mainly British men and women, did their duties faithfully and diligently, without any murmuring or complaints against me. Their attitude and behavior were a good lesson for me.

Another matter of highlight is that I got permission to sign payment checks. Normally, locally appointed accountants did not sign checks. But the consul general in New York obtained special permission from the Treasury Department in London to give me check-signing authority. Every day, I used to sign fifty to a hundred checks. My assistants would bring the printed checks along with the bills or vouchers. I would make sure that everything was correct and then put my signature on it, passing it on to the management officer for his signature. (There is a rule that there should be two signatures for all government-issued checks.) On one occasion, I had the privilege to sign a check for $80 million (that's more than 500 crore rupees in today's exchange rate). That was a matter of great pride for me. I believe that I was given permission to sign checks as an approval of my honest dealings with cash in the past many years.

At this moment, I want to mention a commendation letter our bank manager gave me (without me asking). From the time I joined the office in New York, I would deposit and withdraw large amounts of cash every day. As the amount was large, I never used to count the money at the bank itself. After returning to the office, I'd count the money using a money-counting machine. Three times, I found out there was more money than the check amount (hundreds or even thousands more). All three times, I promptly returned the money to the cashier the next day. I do not know how the manager came to know about it. However, one day, I received a commendation letter from the manager through the cashier. I believe a copy of that letter might have also been sent to our office.

During my service in New York, I dealt with several millions of dollars in cash and checks, and there was never a dollar more or less in the account. I am saying this for the glory of God, that I have been faithful in dealing with millions of dollars. Not only that, but our accounts were also audited every year. I am proud to say that throughout my period as an accountant, we received very good reports from the auditors.

An unusual thing happened. The British Foreign and Commonwealth Office used to produce a diplomats list every three months. As there are over two hundred British posts in the world, only senior diplomats like ambassadors, consuls general, and senior officers were included in it. (For example, we had more than eighty diplomats based in New York, but only twenty diplomats were included in the list). The list used to mention the name, position, and place where they were posted. Every three years, they had to move to new places, so this magazine would reach every British embassy and consulate all over the world, UN mission offices, foreign affairs offices, and other important offices, to keep them up to date of the postings. There were no other names, other than senior British diplomats, in this list. But it was a matter of great pride and miracle that for five years, my name (a non-diplomatic Indian) was included in this list and distributed every three months all over the world. It is a fitting example of God's promise that He lifts those He likes and places them with great and respected leaders. Praise God for His grace and mercy towards me.

Our offices were on the twenty-seventh and twenty-eighth floors of One Dag Hammarskjold Plaza, a sixty-story building on Second Avenue, facing the UN offices and the East River in Manhattan. My office was on the twenty-seventh floor, with a view of the UN building and the East River. The offices were arranged in the order of importance. First the management counselor, second the management officer, and third, the accountant. The management counselor was the head of the Management Department, which managed the affairs of all the British government offices in New York, namely, the mission to the UN, the Consulate General, British trade offices, British Information Services, and the Department of Northern Ireland.

I had two office rooms, one for me, and the one next to mine, for my assistants. One of my friends who visited me in my office told me that in New York, only people with million-dollar salaries would have such an office. When I heard that, I felt proud and thanked God for His grace and blessing. While sitting and working in the office, I could look through the large glass window and see the crowd that comes every day to visit the UN and watch the motorcades that brings high dignitaries to attend the UN General Assembly meetings. Also, I could see the boats and the ships that pass through the East River and the helicopters that fly above the river. These beautiful circumstances made the work so easy and enjoyable.

During this period, Mr. Donald Trump, one of the richest people in America, who later became the president of the United States, bought a piece of property on First Avenue, opposite the UN, and built the tallest and most luxurious apartment building in the world.

From the day the work started, until the completion of the seventy-five-story skyscraper, I could see the modern building techniques used and the daily progress from my office. Because our building was standing on a higher level, and as I was sitting on the twenty-seventh floor, everything was happening below my eye level. It was a great experience and fun to watch the building get completed.

Social gatherings are common in British embassies and other British government offices. In New York, we used to have a cocktail party almost every week. There are so many reasons for it. I think New York is the only city in the world that has an ambassador and a consul general operating. The Consulate, Trade Office, Information Services, and the Northern Ireland offices were operating in another building in Midtown. We handled the accounts for all these departments, and one way or other, almost all the staff members had to deal with me.

As I mentioned earlier, the diplomatic staff used to change every three or four years in these offices. So, we organized a cocktail party to receive and introduce the incoming officers and say farewell to the departing officers. These cocktail parties were held for the delegates to the UN and the delegates to the Disarmament Conferences, the secretary of state and his delegates, the prime minister and his accompanying delegates and officials, naval visits, royal visits, and so on.

Local and British bank managers, government officials, top police officials, FBI officers, UN officials, military advisers to the UN, and some diplomats from other countries were also invited to these high-level parties. Chinnamma and I were also invited to these parties; I could see and get introduced to many high dignitaries. I had the privilege to shake hands with Her Majesty, Queen Elizabeth, her husband, His Highness Prince Phillip, Prime Minister John Major, Secretary of State Douglas Hurd, and Robin Cook. I consider it as a rare privilege and a great achievement.

When Christmas and New Year's arrive, the department heads would take us out to very good restaurants in Manhattan and give us Christmas and New Year treats. The ambassador and counsel general would invite all the staff members to their residence for dinner, on either Christmas or New Years. I had the honor to attend all these dinners. In these dinners, all staff gets equal treatment, from the management counselor to the drivers. Of course, they all came well dressed in suits, and no one took off their shoes in the ambassador's carpeted residence.

These parties were not like the ones we see in films, where people get drunk and make problems. All diplomatic events are conducted in a very decent way. It is true that in all these parties, all kinds of alcoholic drinks are available, and 90 percent of the guests drink it. But in my thirty years of personal experience of attending these parties, I have never seen anyone get drunk and misbehave. Someone once asked me if I was a Muslim, when he saw me drinking soft drinks only. Many people believe that all Christians drink alcohol. It is a shameful thing that some of our people get drunk, even misbehaving on an airplane.

While talking about parties, I think it's not inappropriate to mention my retirement party. Between Doha and New York, I had worked for thirty years with the British government. I also worked about ten years in the private sector between Bombay and Doha. Even though there were about four more years for my normal retirement, I had some feeling in my mind that it was time to stop. I mentioned it to Chinnamma, and she said she felt the same way, as she too had worked as a nurse for forty years. Both our daughters had finished their studies and were married. Not only that, my parents and Chinnamma's parents had passed away. So, our financial responsibility was less. That is why we thought of taking early retirement when we turned sixty-two. Because of my good job and our good salaries, we were a bit hesitant to make the decision. My only concern was that once I retired, I wouldn't be able to contribute for the Gospel work and help the poor people, as much as I used to in the past.

While we were in this state of confusion, Chinnamma suddenly became very sick. She had a ruptured appendix, which we only learned after her whole body became septic. Because she had chronic diabetes, she didn't feel any pain. When she got a high fever, she went to her doctor, and he sent her straight to the hospital. They said it was too late, but after two surgeries and more than thirty days in the hospital, she was discharged. By the grace of God and prayers of many saints, she got her life back, but the doctor said she wouldn't be the same as before. Chinnamma was completely broken, physically and emotionally. That was a turning point in our life.

While she was in the hospital, she wasn't thinking properly and said she would stop working; she also asked me to resign, as she would need my care and assistance all the time. I submitted my resignation, but as the accountant, they did not want to release me right away. But when I explained that my family had a problem that was more important than the job, the management counselor was kind enough to call the Treasury Department in London, and they gave permission to accept my resignation.

Before my final departure from the office, they arranged a big farewell party for me. Special invitations were printed on official British government cards, and more than two hundred fifty guests were invited, all British and American nationals except for my wife, myself, my daughter Jean and her husband, Tom Benson, my daughter Judy and her husband, Jacob Mathews, and their son Michael; and a cousin of mine, Mini Shaji. Almost all of the staff members, some banking officials, and other contacts were invited. After a few farewell and congratulatory speeches, the office staff gave me a gift, and then, the management counselor presented me a special gift. When I opened it, I felt surprised and very happy. It was a framed certificate of my thirty years of loyal service to the British government, signed by Secretary of State Honorable Robin Cook. It was sent, in a diplomatic bag, from London to reach here in time for the farewell party. In fact, when I left Doha, I had resigned from my job, and my New York appointment was only a local appointment. Even then, without my asking, the foreign minister of the British government issued me a certificate of appreciation for my thirty years of loyal service. I was so thankful to the foreign minister and the Lord for lifting me up. I remembered the verse that said God will honor the ones that honor him, and I thanked and praised Him. After my words of thanks, many hugged and kissed me with a heavy heart and bid farewell to me. Chinnamma's office also gave her a grand farewell party.

Thus, my service with the British government came to an end. I started at Doha, Qatar, in 1970 and ended it in New York in 2000. These were the most satisfying years in my life. I thank the British government for allowing me, an Indian, to serve them for thirty years, without any discrimination. I also sincerely thank the members of the Foreign Services I worked with. Hundreds of them, including ten ambassadors, five consuls general, and other high officials, all treated me with love, respect, and special consideration. I greatly appreciate that all of them worked with me with no regard for me being an Indian. They all sincerely encouraged my progress and betterment. I consider it as a grace of God towards me that the country that ruled India for more than two centuries treated me with care and love. I thank God for that.

I humbly admit that I am a debtor to the Lord and my Savior Jesus Christ forever. I give Him all glory, praises, and adoration. I am also waiting for His Second Coming.

At this time, I also sincerely thank my dear wife, Chinnamma, who stood with me in all my endeavors. She helped me with love and care in all my efforts and needs. She was the reason for me to go to the gulf and to the US. And it was through Chinnamma that God gave me two beautiful girls, two smart sons-in-law, and two blessed grandsons. It is also true that Chinnamma was an important factor in our happy family life. Once again, I thank God for all His grace and provisions.

Time kept going, and a few more years went by. In 2000, we both took early retirement, as arranged by God. As per our age, we both could have worked for another four or five years. But we had worked forty years each in our life and thought there was no point in working until we fell dead. We were very confident that the Lord, who took care of us thus far, would take care of us in the future also, even through Chinnamma's sickness. I think God helped us make this decision. Therefore, we decided to spend the rest of our life thanking and praising the Lord for His blessings and living for His glory. We also committed ourselves to God to use us according to His will and for His glory.

About ten years after my retirement, I was sitting at home and remembered that many people asked me to write down my memoirs; I thought it might glorify God's name if I shared the countless blessings, He showered upon me. It may encourage readers and draw them closer to God. That is why I am writing down my memories of His grace and shepherding to me.

CHAPTER 7

Deposit for Eternity

I have no doubt that some people may have different opinions about what I am going to say below. You might say I am writing these things for self-praise and therefore will lose my eternal rewards. But I understand that the good Lord said when people do things in public for self-praise, they already received their reward.

But if someone does something in private, out of kindness or the love of God, its reward is immediately deposited in the heavenly treasury. Later on, if it's revealed in public, it can encourage others to repeat it. If you have done something in the love of God and for His glory, there is no doubt that you will get appreciation and blessings, in this world and the world to come. That is why the story of the widow who put in one penny is mentioned in the Bible. Also, we read about apostles Peter and Paul, who gave themselves up for God's work. They did all that because of their love of God, not for praise. Their rewards are already recorded in heaven. They did not do it for their glory at that time, but unless it is recorded and made known to us, how can we appreciate it and follow their good works? If it is not revealed, nobody gets benefited, and by revealing it, I don't think their rewards will be reduced or removed. We have always tried to follow the footsteps of our predecessors, especially in the matter of giving and doing good works. When I consider myself, I know what I did is nothing compared to what others did, but I am happy and proud of what I have done, from my limited resources.

Some of these matters are things I did forty to fifty years ago. I did these things out of my love for God. At that time, I did not know

I would live this long or write a memoir. No doubt, I myself have been influenced by other people's policies and good works. Similarly, if people read about my good work, and I can influence them to follow my path, it will benefit Gospel work and bring glory to God. Then, I will be very pleased. I don't have any big things to report, but just like that widow, whatever I did from my limited circumstances, and my testimony of His faithfulness to me, would definitely glorify God's name.

Though I was born again at the age of ten, I was a lukewarm believer until the age of thirty. It is a fact that even in those days, I loved and feared God. After getting married and landing a good job in Doha, I started a closer and committed life with God. Friendship with good people and fellowship with the children of God in Doha also influenced me. I am also glad to say that visiting Brethren preachers and Pentecostal evangelists influenced me to make a more committed spiritual life.

After my arrival in Bombay, I had about five years of very happy spiritual fellowship with the Pentecostal church in Chembur. My sister, brother-in-law, and I were born Brethren people and members of the Brethren Assembly in Kerala. But it was impossible for my brother-in-law, living in Chembur, to go to the Brethren Assembly in Fort. At the same time, there were several loving, caring, and spiritually active people gathering in a Pentecostal church in Chembur. My sister and brother-in-law participated, as a matter of convenience. As I was staying with them, I naturally joined them. Soon after, they convinced me of the need to get baptized. They urged me to get baptized as early as possible and told me that nobody keeps a dead body for long; they bury it as soon as possible. When I was in Kerala, I knew I had to get baptized, but nobody in our assembly encouraged me at that time.

When Pastor P. M. Phillip returned from an American visit, Brother T. M. Simon and I got baptized under his hand in the sea, near Juhu Beach. In those days, I was really enjoying spiritual life and fellowship. One night, Brother Simon and I and some other believers spent hours in an open field, praying to receive the gift of speaking in other tongues, but I did not receive any new language.

All the believers in that church were very close to each other, and I established good friendships with many. Even after many years, I had the privilege to renew my friendship in the US with dear Pastor Mathew Samuel, K. V. Kurian, Thomas Koshy, and Pappachen and K. C. Cherian.

After we arrived in Doha, we went to the Catholic church there for a few weeks, due to the pressure from Chinnamma. I had no interest in attending the Catholic church, but I had a burning desire to bring my Catholic wife to the brethren beliefs and its fellowship. I had been earnestly praying for that. God heard my prayer and brought a few brethren believers into our house. Some of them were from our own native place and members of our own assembly in Ranny. Their love, prayers, and gentle invitation changed Chinnamma's mind, and she agreed to go with me to the Brethren Assembly.

That was a turning point in our spiritual life. God did not allow us to ever turn back on that decision. Chinnamma had earlier heard the Gospel through Brother M. E. Cherian when he visited Doha, and she had accepted Jesus Christ as her personal Savior. In early 1970s, a few pastors and evangelists visited Doha and gave glorious messages. After these messages and personal dealings, Chinnamma decided on a water baptism. On our next trip to India, Chinnamma was baptized under the hands of evangelist K. K. Chacko, from Kottayam. Praise God.

After a few years, there was a split in the Doha Brethren Assembly. In 1974, with the arrival of a Bible scholar and a good preacher, Oommen George, along with Elder Chackochan, K. C. Mathew, A. G. George, and others, we started a new gathering in the name of Ebenezer Brethren Assembly. For the first few years, the gathering was at my house due to space availability, and it was known under my address until 1983, when I left Doha. During that period, we were able to show hospitality to visiting evangelists, including Nina Pillai. In addition, when the Christian ship *Logos* visited Doha, I was able to invite a few of the officers from the ship to my home and entertain them.

Even after coming to New York, we had the privilege to entertain many evangelists in our home. It is a matter of great joy that even in my house in Ranny, Kerala, many evangelists were accommodated and taken care of. For that matter, my parents and my sister and brother-in-law were also very keen to serve the children of God.

In the early 1970s, I started sending financial help to a few brothers in Kerala and some evangelists in north India. This amount increased every year, and I helped evangelists working in north India, as listed in the KEM Fund list. Later, God enabled me to send financial assistance to everyone on the KEM list, including evangelists from Kerala. By the grace of God, I helped evangelists for the next twenty-five years, until I retired from work. Not only that but in one particular year, I was also on top of the individual contributors from all over the world, listed through the KEM Fund. I am not saying this for my own praise but for the glory of God, for enabling this humble servant to do it. This is mentioned to encourage others and for my self-satisfaction. I noticed that in later days, it has worked out as I desired, resulting in many blessings. I am happy with that result and may God's name be glorified through others also.

After migrating to the US, I was involved with many spiritual activities. I took responsibilities in our local church and on the national level, as a committee member in the Northeastern Conference and for youth retreats, GMI, and FIBA. By the grace of God, He raised me up to be an elder and president of our local assembly, India Gospel Assembly in New York. God enables me to take Word ministry and Bible studies in our local church. We, as a family, used to undertake the ministry of prayer. After retirement, my wife and I spent hours in prayer for others and for the salvation of the perishing souls.

All the members of Chinnamma's large family are Roman Catholics. So with a burden in heart, we used to pray for them. After more than twenty-five years of continuous prayers, I am glad to say that several people from her family have accepted Jesus Christ as their personal Savior. It was all God's doing, and we are very happy about it. I have been able to lead a number of our family friends to the saving knowledge of God. There are a few more who accepted Jesus Christ through me, during our home-to-home Gospel ministry, along with a number of evangelists and the Aluva Church members in Kerala. Altogether, over thirty people have accepted Jesus Christ through me. God worked in their hearts and used me as an instrument. It was not due to my smartness, but none of them joined our assembly. Even then, I am happy that those people have become children of God and heirs to the heavenly Kingdom. I consider this as my greatest achievement and wealth in my life, and I plead to God to enable me to rescue a few more from eternal condemnation. While giving millions of thanks to God for what He has accomplished through me, I pray that the redeemed ones should obey the Lord's commandment and be in fellowship of God's people.

When I was working in Manhattan, I had an hour for lunch. There was a lot of free time after I ate. I used to walk through the sidewalks and the entrance of nearby subways and hand over hundreds of gospel tracts and Bible portions to the people going by. In addition, whenever we were touring foreign countries, I carried a few copies of the Gospel tracts and Bible portions with me and hand them over to the people there. I was able to do this in Brazil, Argentina, Australia, New Zealand, Tahiti, China, Russia, and South Africa. I remember when several of our church members were on a journey to Communist China, we got permission of the officers on the ship and conducted a Sunday worship meeting; many staff members keenly observed our service. We were even able to share the Gospel with a few people there. There were occasions when I had to wait long hours at the airports for my next flight. I took courage and handed out Gospel tracts and Bible portions to tired and anxious passengers as well as some stall attendants. I did all these things out of my love for the Lord and my concern for the perishing souls.

Nearly fifteen years ago, I became a member of the Gideons International, a Christian organization. They have local camps in nearly two hundred countries, and they have thousands of men and women members working with them. They print millions of full Bibles and New Testaments in many languages and distribute them all over the world. I had the privilege to distribute thousands of Bibles to school students, hospitals, old age homes, hotels, colleges, and the general public. At present, I am the vice president of our local camp in Long Island, New York. Moreover, I have sponsored thousands of New Testament Bibles to be delivered to the people of poor countries. All Bibles are given free everywhere, and thousands of people have become children of God through this work.

In addition, I had the privilege to sponsor sending hundreds of Bibles to Communist China, through the American Bible Society. I was also able to distribute a few Bibles in Kerala, through Brother P. P. George (Ankamali). I did all these things to save souls and for the glory of God. There is no doubt that the good Lord will reward me for all these services. Another ministry I've done in recent years is conducting a number of one-day seminars with evangelists and their families in different parts of Kerala and Tamil Nadu. The first one was in Madurai, arranged by Brother James Cherian. About fifty evangelists and their families attended, and after the seminar, food and financial help were provided.

Similarly, a year later, about forty evangelists and their families from the districts of Cannanoor and Kazerkode were treated to a seminar, where food and financial support were provided. The next year, about fifty evangelists and their families from the districts of Wayand, Kozikode, and Malapuram were treated the same way. A year later, more than fifty evangelists and their families from the district of Palakkad were treated to a one-day seminar. This was in conjunction with the Erikum Chira Assembly monthly meeting. More than two hundred people were given food, and financial help to all the evangelists. These were all very blessed occasions. In all these cases, Jojo P. J., an evangelist from Aluva, assisted me in organizing these seminars and transporting me to these places.

Just like with spiritual matters, both my wife and I were keen to help the needy and poor as much as we could. We did all these things from our limited resources and the blessings God has given us. I am sure the young generation can do many times more than me from the abundance of the Lord's blessings. About fifty years ago, I decided to give 10 percent of my income for God's work and good works. I thank God for enabling me to fulfill that promise all these years. It is a fact that in some years, I was able to exceed that target.

When I was working, God enabled me to extend a helping hand to over four hundred evangelists listed in KEM Fund list. For many years, I was able to help the evangelists in north India on a continuous basis. Even when I was in Doha, I made it a point to be the top contributor for our assembly.

I am not telling all this to show how much I paid; no doubt, I am very happy and satisfied for what I did in the past, but my main interest is to inspire the young generation to give generously, even with a competitive mind, to the work of God so more evangelists can be supported and carry out more Gospel work. The new generation these days have salaries three to four times that of our days, because of their better jobs due to their higher education. I am praying to God to give them a good heart and a burden to give.

When I retired, I was able to set aside a portion of my benefits for God's work and have spent it for that purpose over the past fifteen years. There is great joy in giving. I know it is difficult for the old generation to give big amounts for God's work. I hope the new generation follows my example. From my own experience, I can proudly say that you will lack nothing by giving to God's work and helping the poor and needy.

Helping the needy is also important to Chinnamma, just like me. She took the initiative to sponsor a girl who had no means for higher education, meeting all her expenses for a nursing course. She completed her nursing studies and is now working in England as a staff nurse. You know how happy she and her family are? So are we.

I had the privilege to sponsor two houses for poor believers through the Believer's Relief Trust. In 2002, I was able to provide a number of sewing machines to provide a sustainable income to poor ladies through Precious Life Ministry. I helped a poor young man buy an auto rickshaw, as he had no job or any income. This gave him a job and a means of livelihood. He later sold it and bought a secondhand taxi car. It gave us (and that young boy and his family) great joy. When I was in the gulf, I had the opportunity to bring some people there, without taking any money from them. Now, they and their family members are well settled there, and their joy and gratitude for what we have done for them are overwhelming.

For us, we have lasting happiness and rewards in heaven for the good works we have done here. That is a promise of God, and He will not fail to do it. We may lose what we accumulate here for us, and sometimes, we may not be able to enjoy it. We regret and worry about it for long, as we won't get it back. Whereas, if you give a portion of your blessings to God's work and the poor, it will never be a loss, as God will bless you more, and you will have deposits in heaven.

In the past few years, I had the privilege to lend a helping hand to several students in our assembly in Kerala. Also, for the last five years, I was able to sponsor ten evangelists and their families for their medical insurance coverage. This has helped many of them in their very difficult times, may God's name be glorified. Similarly, for the last twenty years, I have been contributing to a dozen charitable organizations here in the US that lend a helping hand to the uprooted and needy all over the world. The main ones are the American Red Cross, Care International, Food for the Hungry, and others that reach out to help people in earthquakes, floods, tsunami, droughts, and so on.

In 1982, the former American president, Jimmy Carter, started a charitable organization called the Carter Center, which helps undeveloped and poor African nations with medicine, agricultural tools, seeds, and so on. I have been a part of it for nearly twenty years. I participated in other organizations, like Teen Challenge, which tries to save alcoholics and drug addicts, and other research organizers who tried to find cures for cancer, Alzheimer's, and so on.

By lending a small hand in all these activities, we feel that we are part of the good works, and we also benefit from their goodness. These simple acts give us great satisfaction in our life. It's a matter of great joy that over the years, I have been able to donate one gallon of my blood to save others' lives. I don't take any credit for any of these actions. It was all by the grace of God. He gave me the resources, good health, and a sympathetic heart to love and help others. Let His name be glorified.

I thank God for enabling me to make a small contribution in the area of Christian literature. I never had any special interest or aptitude in writing. In fact, I was not even a good reader of books, but I used to enjoy listening to the songs and music. After my retirement at the age of sixty-one, God gave me the ability to create literary compositions. I spent many hours a day, for many years, in long hours of prayer and in the study of the Bible. Then, six years into my retirement, God gave me the ability to write the lyrics of a Christian song.

I wrote my first song at the age of sixty-eight. In the following three years, I wrote more than fifty Malayalam Christian songs. Some of them were published in Christian magazines, and a few of them were presented at conferences. Later, I was able to write a few songs in English and one song in Hindi. During the period between 2010 and 2020, three CDs were recorded, comprising forty of my songs. One or two songs among them became very popular among the Kerala evangelists, who do the open-air Gospel works. I am glad they are being used for the glory of God and for the propagation of the Gospel.

Based on the events and the truths in the Bible, God gave me the grace to write a few poems, which I presented it to the Christian community in the form of a book. *Kristheeya Kavitha Manjary* (Christian Poems) was written in Malayalam and includes the following poems:

1. *Deivathinte Karyaparipadical* (God's Plan and Programs). This contains the Creation, the people of Israel, and Christ and the way of Salvation, based on Genesis, Exodus, and the Gospels of Matthew, Mark, Luke, and John.
2. *Eyobin Kastangal, Nastangal, Nettangal* (The Sufferings, Losses, and Achievements of Job). This is taken from the book of Job.
3. *Puthen Yerusalem* (New Jerusalem). This is the hope of the children of God and their eternal heavenly home, which is described in the book of Revelation.

After that, I wrote a few more poems and published them in the name of *Khristiya Kavita Manjeri Part 2* (Christian Poems Part 2). The following poems are there:

1. *Jeevante Vachanam* (The Word of Life)
2. *Khristuvilulla Raksha* (Salvation through Christ)

3. *Kristuvum Sabhayum* (Christ and the Church, based on Songs of Solomon and Revelation)
4. *Utthamayaya Bharya* (The Ideal Wife, based on Proverbs 31)
5. *Kannya Mariam* (Virgin Mary, based on the Gospel of Matthew)
6. *Magdalana Mariam* (Mary Magdalene, based on the Gospels)
7. *Onesimus* (Onesimus, based on the book of Philemon)
8. *Ninavayude Veendedup* (Redemption of Nineveh, based on the book of Jonah)
9. *Ruth* (Ruth, based on the book of Ruth)
10. *Kristhu Chaitha Alpudhngal* (The Miracles of Jesus, based on Gospels
11. *Solomanum Sulemkarariyum* (Solomon and the Shulamite, based on the Song of Songs and the Song of Solomon)
12. *Daveed Rajav* (King David, based on 1 and 2 Samuel)
13. *Purim Festival* (The Story of Esther)

I wrote five other nonbiblical poems: *Sambathika Mannyam* (The Declining Economy), *Abhayam* (Refuge), *Kaalangal Marumbol* (Seasonal Changes in American Trees), and *New Yorkile Manju Veeshcha* (Snowfall in New York).

In 2012, based on these poems, I received a literary award from the Bible Literature Forum, in Houston, Texas. I am grateful to them and to God for His blessings in this field.

CHAPTER 8

*In Search of the Borders of the **World***

In this age of Internet, discovery, Google, and travel channels, I do not intend to describe places, countries, cultures, or other details. Anybody can find these details through the above media, better described than I can do. I just want to mention the places we visited, the things we saw and liked, and our own experiences in these places.

After joining the British Embassy in Doha, every two years, we used to visit Kerala and spend two months with my parents, friends, and family. By the time we returned to Kerala in 1976, God helped us to build a fairly large and beautiful two-story house in the prime area of Ranny Town. My father supervised its construction. My parents and I moved into that new house, and I also bought a brand-new Ambassador car for their use. We enrolled both of our children in boarding school in Mavelikara. Having accomplished that much in life, we decided to travel to places we had not seen. Both Chinnamma and I had an interest in traveling.

Even though we had visited London twice, we had not taken any organized tours before. So, in 1979, we decided to take a tour of Europe and the US: fifteen days in Europe and forty-five days in America.

Rome, Paris, London, New York, Washington

Our first stop was in Rome, Italy. We stayed there for a few days and took daily tours arranged by the hotel. We saw the Roman Coliseum, which is one of the wonders of the world. We saw it in all detail, inside and outside, including the broken places, climbed on top of the high walls and enjoyed the view from there, and were amazed at the beautiful architecture and its construction more than two thousand years ago. We also visited the Roman Forum, Novena Square, the Altar of the Nation, beautiful Tivoli Gardens, and many other interesting places. Also, we saw the Vatican City, historical churches, and the place where Apostle Paul was held as a prisoner. Then we saw Saint Peter's Square, Saint Peter's Church, the world-famous paintings of Michelangelo, Villa Borghese, and so on. All these sites were very delightful.

After Rome, we went to Paris, where we saw many interesting and beautiful places. We were so happy to visit the world-famous Eiffel Tower and go on top of the tower and see the city from all four angles. Then we took a bus tour that visited the Arc de Triomphe, Palace of Versailles, the East Garden, and more. The tour buses in Rome and Paris were luxurious and air conditioned. Not only that but the tour guide's comments were translated into ten languages. In 1979, all those things were new experiences to us, and we both were delighted.

After finishing our tours of Paris by boat and at night, we saw what a modern world it was. But eating is rather difficult in Paris. Food is very costly, and it was difficult to order anything, as the menu is only in French, and the waiters won't speak English. I was told they were proud people, and even if they knew English, they wouldn't speak it. And if you have to use the public toilet, you have to put in coins to open the door. It was difficult to carry the right coins because we could not read French.

After Paris, we went to London. As we had been there previously we knew what to do and where to go and how to go. From the tourist information materials available in the embassy, I knew by heart the places of interest, the underground system, and so on. As the UK was promoting tourism, all information was easily available everywhere we were.

We walked, took the double-decker tourist bus and underground trains, and saw almost all the important tourist attractions: Buckingham Palace, changing of the guards, House of Parliament, Westminster

Abbey, Trafalgar Square, Piccadilly Circus, Tower Bridge, Crown Jewels in the Tower, Saint Paul's Cathedral, British Museum, and London Zoo. We took a boat journey on River Thames and saw other interesting things. One of the Crown Jewels was the Kohinoor Diamond, which was from India. We saw Madame Tussaud's Wax Museum. It was a wonder for us at that time period. The lifelike full-size figures of the British Royal family, Mahatma Gandhi, Indira Gandhi, and other world leaders and famous people looked so real in size, color, and appearance. We also visited the prime minister's residence at 10 Downing Street and the Queen's private residence at Windsor Castle. I took a chance and attended a football game at the world-famous Wembley Stadium. We both were very happy and satisfied at our tour achievements. I felt so attached to London as I was an employee of the British government. Altogether, London is a beautiful and interesting place.

After the London visit, we flew to the US. A few months earlier, Chinnamma's younger brother and family had immigrated to America. They were staying in New Jersey, where her elder brother, Reverend Dr. Matthew Adackapara, had bought a house for them. His church's parsonage was nearby. We visited many places in the US, having our base in New Jersey. I was amazed at the size and beauty of Manhattan and New York City. It was the first time in my life that I saw such skyscrapers and so many huge bridges, like Verrazano and George Washington Bridges. When I looked up to the top of the buildings, standing at the bottom, my neck used to ache. It was a great joy to go to the top of the tallest building in the world, the Twin Towers (World Trade Center), the Empire State Building, and the Statue of Liberty. When we look down from the top of the World Trade Center, the cars below looked like small toys and people looked like matchsticks. It was so nice to see the beautiful Rockefeller Center and the UN buildings. I took a special pass to see the inside of the UN General Assembly Hall, UN Security Council, and the tall Office Tower.

Similarly, we visited Washington and took a detailed tour of the White House, Capitol Building, Washington Monument, Smithsonian Institute, National Air Space Museum, and Arlington

National Cemetery, where President John F. Kennedy is buried. We also had a glimpse of the Pentagon and Lincoln Center from outside. We also visited Hartford and nearby places in Connecticut. We visited Independence Hall and the Liberty Bell in Philadelphia and that beautiful city. There were many interesting places in New Jersey also. The luxurious casinos in Atlantic City and the beautiful beaches like Sandy Hook were also exciting and satisfying places.

We also saw many Malayalee friends. There was a good number of our own family and relatives in these areas. Compared to the small kingdoms in the gulf, the US was so big, so advanced, and full of different cultures and people from all over the world. There were no restrictions like we had in the Gulf States. Most people didn't have much savings, and many were in debt, but the Americans led a luxurious and happy life. Not only that but the immigrants could bring their parents, siblings, and others, and the children had a better chance for higher education and a better future.

We also had the opportunity to get to know the brethren believers and their churches here. They had full freedom to establish their own churches and worship God anywhere, unlike the Gulf States.

When we saw all these things, our previous attitude changed, and we desired to come and live here. That was when we asked Chinnamma's elder brother to file an immigration application for us.

On July 2, 1983, we arrived here as immigrants to live on a permanent basis. Following that, we all got busy with the children's education and Chinnamma's further studies. As I got a job within a month, I got busy with my job also. And then, as I had planned while in Doha, my parents got visiting visas to come here, and I arranged for them to be here in the summer of 1984. They came here and stayed with us for three months. During that period, we took them to many interesting places in New York, Washington, Philadelphia, and New Jersey. We also visited a number of our family members, which made them very happy.

Niagara and Toronto, Canada

My parents went with us to see the world-famous and wonderful Niagara Falls. We all were very happy to see this God-made wonder, and we thanked Him. Similarly, Toronto is a very beautiful city. Its clean and beautiful parks, boat jetty, and the tall CN Tower are all delightful. From far, the CN Tower looks like a pillar, but when you come close, it is so big and tall. About five hundred feet up on the top, there is a revolving restaurant, and above that, there is a very high antenna to broadcast radio and television signals. We all went in and up to the top and saw everything in detail, and we were fully satisfied and delighted before we returned to New York. It was also there, for the first time, in my life, I saw an amphitheater.

In 1985, we did not go on any long tour but were content to travel nearby and attend an Ohio Brethren Conference.

In 1986, we decided to visit India. During the children's summer vacation, we went to Kerala, after visiting Bombay. It was so nice to see my parents, sisters, their families, and other dear ones. During our visit, it was my birthday. My mother took special interest to celebrate it, and without my knowledge, she arranged a birthday cake through my father and prepared special food for the occasion. It was well celebrated.

After that, we visited Chinnamma's family and had a very happy get-together. Then we visited the famous Idukki Arch Dam, Malambuza Dam and its beautiful park, and Thekkady Wildlife Reserve, where we took a boat ride in the reservoir.

But sad to say, two weeks before our return flight, my mother had a heart attack. On that day, for a long period of time, my wife and I were talking to my parents in their bedroom on the lower floor. We were all sitting on two beds that were in that room. It was time for dinner, and the servant girl came and informed us that the dinner was ready. Therefore, Chinnamma and I moved to the dining table. Ammachi, my mother, said she didn't want to eat. We were about to start our dinner, then my father called out to me saying my mother was not well. I was told that as soon as we moved to the dining room, my mother fell back onto the bed. In less than a minute, we were in the bedroom, but by that time, she had gone. Chinnamma, a nurse, checked her pulse and breathing, but both had stopped. We were all shocked, but gaining courage, Chinnamma and I gave her CPR and revived her. Her breathing and pulse started working again. As directed, my father immediately went out to bring a doctor from the nearby hospital, which was five minutes' walking distance.

Within fifteen minutes, he returned with a doctor. But all that he had with him was a stethoscope. He checked her, said it was a heart attack, and told us to take her to the hospital. As it was about nine in the evening, our driver had gone home, and I couldn't drive at that moment. So, the doctor himself volunteered to drive, and we took her in his car. We were in the back seat, her head in my lap and her legs in my dad's lap. Because she made some noise with her breathing, we knew she was alive. Within five minutes, we were at the hospital casualty section. As soon as we reached there, she stopped breathing. Immediately, the doctor ran out and brought back a needle that he injected directly into her heart. But he could not revive her. I thought about the fully equipped ambulance service in the US, and the ill-equipped hospitals in Ranny at that time. But I couldn't do anything but grieve.

When we moved to the USA from Doha, Ammachi had been concerned about the distance in case of an emergency, but when it really happened, I was right there, and she passed away lying in my lap. That was my only comfort and consolation. For her funeral, my sisters, brothers-in-law, and some grandchildren came from Bombay and Doha. My father was now alone, and as he didn't want to come and stay with me in New York, I requested my elder sister Thankamma and her husband, who had retired from Air India, to come and stay with my father, and they gracefully accepted. Thus, we went back to the US with peace of mind.

Florida, Disney World, Texas, Oklahoma

Next year, we decided to take the children to Disney World. My wife's brother and family also joined us. So, Chinnamma and I, Jean and Judy, and Appachen, Leelamma, and their four children flew to Orlando and stayed in a hotel there. We rented a large van and drove together to Epcot Center, Disney World, and many other places of interest. The lighted character parade at night was especially interesting. We also enjoyed several spectacular and frightening rides there. From there, we went to Fort Lauderdale and Miami, visiting their world-famous and beautiful beaches.

In 1988, we visited Houston, Dallas, and Oklahoma. From Houston, we were driving to Dallas in the car of Alex and Kunjumol, my nephew's in-laws. Chinnamma and my elder sister Thankamma were also in the car. It was a rainy day, and there was hardly any traffic on the highway. After a stopover at a resting place, I took over the driving, and as the road was free, I was driving at about 75 miles per hour. The road was wet, and a light rain was still falling. Suddenly, our car spun out and turned over two to three times, landing in a swampy place in three to four feet of water. Luckily and by the grace of God, the car landed on its wheels. As it was a high-speed highway and hardly any traffic, no one saw us land in the swamp. The car got stuck in the mud, and we could not open the door. Alex slid down the window a little, called the police, and explained the situation. The police came and called a tow truck, which pulled us out of the swamp. As it was a strong Volvo car, and the doors were locked, we were not thrown out. But all of us had bruises and pain all over the body for several days. If the car had landed upside down in the swamp, all five of us would have drowned. It was God's love and abundant grace that we all escaped from that very dangerous accident. A million thanks to my loving Lord and God. The police told us we had hydroplaned on the wet road. It was the first time I heard that word.

In Dallas, we saw where President John F. Kennedy was assassinated. In Oklahoma, we visited the Oral Roberts Ministry Center. On another visit, we saw the Oklahoma City Federal Building bombing site and the National Memorial established in remembrance of the victims. I found the engineering of the roads around Dallas very interesting.

In addition to visiting these places, we saw many of our friends and relatives in these three states. During the next several years, we were able to visit forty out of the fifty American states. Each state has something different and interesting to offer.

Los Angeles, San Diego, and Tijuana, Mexico

Next year, we decided to visit California and the West Coast. Our friends Baby Mathew and his wife Elsie Mathew also joined us. In California, we visited Los Angeles, Napa Valley, and a few huge vineyards and wine distilleries. It was the first time I saw such large vineyards. We saw the Crystal Palace, Disneyland, and the world-famous Los Angeles beaches. From there we hired a car and went down to San Diego and to the Mexican border city of Tijuana. While in San Diego, we visited the large aquarium there and saw Shamu, the large whale.

Catalina

From Los Angeles, we went on a large boat to Catalina Island, a tourist attraction. It was a beautiful place with beaches, hills, and valleys. It was a small city. It had a chocolate-making factory and a lot of wild bison. Bison meat products were a specialty there. We went around and saw the places and also ate some bison meat. Then we decided to return to Los Angeles. But by the time we reached the jetty, the last boat of the day had left. So we had to spend the night there and return to the mainland next morning. But it was impossible to get a hotel room that night. The hotel rooms had all been booked in advance. With much searching and persuasion, one room was given for two couples. We had no changes of clothing, and all four of us spent the night on one bed, barely sleeping. Early the next morning, we took the first boat available and returned to Los Angeles. Luckily, we could see a number of large whales on our boat journey.

Bombay, Mysore, Bangalore, Kerala

Also in 1989, we went to India and visited Bombay, Mysore, Bangalore, and Kerala. As my sisters lived in Bombay, every time we went on leave to Kerala, we also visited Bombay and spent a few days with my sisters. I also visited some of my old friends there. We visited many interesting places in Mysore and Bangalore. Mysore Palace and Brindavan Gardens were very interesting. Bangalore was not very advanced at that time.

Since then, there have been many changes and progress in Bangalore. In January 1991, we visited Kerala, and in September of the same year, we went to Kerala again, in connection with my father's death.

The Bahamas and Nassau

Many of our British diplomatic staff going on vacation to the UK used luxury cruise liners like *Queen Mary II* instead of flying. They gave very high opinions of these journeys. When I heard it from many, I thought I should try one of these ships. So, Chinnamma and I booked a cruise on Carnival, going to the Bahamas and Nassau. It was our first journey on a cruise liner, and everything was new and exciting to us. It was a very good experience, and we enjoyed every bit of that visit.

The ship was eleven stories high, with six large lifts. Each one of them could carry about twenty passengers at a time. There were more than two thousand passengers and a thousand workers in it. There were two large swimming pools and recreation areas, one large sauna, a fully equipped gym, twenty-four-hour restaurants and huge dining places, specialty restaurants, beauty parlors, bars, a casino, a cinema, and entertainment areas. Two dining rooms that could accommodate about a thousand people at a time served six-course lunches and dinners. Altogether, the ship was a small modern city.

It was my first-time seeing paragliding in the Bahamas. A boat took you into the sea and connected you to a large balloon, like a parachute, and the boat moved at high speed into the sea. Then the balloon lifted you very high. After flying high on this balloon for a few minutes, the balloon is brought back to the boat. I found it interesting and wanted to take a ride on it, but Chinnamma wouldn't let me, as she was afraid.

During the next two years, three of my sisters and brothers-in-law, a niece and her husband, and a few our friends in Doha visited us. I was able to show them around New York City, Washington, and other interesting places.

New Delhi, Agra, and Taj Mahal

In 1995, while on leave in India, we visited New Delhi and the world-famous Taj Mahal in Agra. Taj Mahal was so beautiful in architecture and its workmanship. We also visited the Red Fort, Kuttab Minar, the Parliament building, and many other interesting places. The Lotus Temple was also very beautiful.

Chicago, San Francisco, Reno, and Virginia

Next year, we did a lot of traveling. We went to Toronto to attend a wedding. We used that opportunity to visit a few friends in Canada. Afterwards, we went to Chicago, a large city like New York. There are many skyscrapers in Chicago like the Sears Tower, the second tallest building in the US. We went on top of it and enjoyed the panoramic view of Chicago. We also visited the world-famous Moody Bible Institute and saw videos promoting the Gospel in America and all over the world. It was very interesting and encouraging, and I thank God for that.

San Francisco was very interesting. The trains went up and down its many hills. Then we went to Reno, which is a small town in Nevada. But a lot of tourists visit there, as there are several casinos. As we walked through the airport, people were playing coin-operated slot machines. The noise of coins falling, and people's excitement took us to a wonderland. We also had the opportunity to visit Lake Tahoe and took a boat on the lake, along with our family friend Rani. In the same year, we also visited Virginia and saw many important places, like the beautiful Virginia Caverns.

Israel and Greece

In the year of 1996 itself, we went to Israel and Greece. It was a very interesting trip, as we were in a group of about forty-five people, comprising of our friends and church members. It was arranged by our friend and neighbor, Baby Mathews. On the way, we had a stopover in Athens, Greece. We took a tour around the city and saw the ancient Parthenon temple and the first Olympic stadium. We also saw the rock in the Areopagus hills, on which apostle Paul stood and preached to the Greeks. I was able to stand on that rock and praise God. That filled my heart with joy.

In Israel, we visited many sites, starting with Jesus Christ's birthplace to the place of His Crucifixion, and even the place from where he ascended into heaven. I was thrilled when I walked through the same path that Jesus walked, and to see the empty tomb where he was buried. Then we saw the Jordan River and took a boat journey on the Sea of Galilee. When we stood at the Wailing Wall, we felt the Bible stories and the Gospel were right in front of our eyes. Jerusalem, the Upper Room, the Golden Temple, Masada, the Dead Sea, and Tel Aviv will ever remain in our memories. Floating on the waters of the Dead Sea was a great experience and good memory. Seeing the Golan Heights, Jericho, Bethlehem, and other sites in Israel made our faith in Christianity stronger.

Vancouver and Victoria in Canada

In 1997, we visited Vancouver, a beautiful city on the west coast of Canada. On that trip, we also visited Victoria, the capital of British Columbia. That place is very beautiful. In Vancouver, we attended the wedding of my cousin's son. The wedding ceremony and reception party were quite different from what I had attended in the US.

Las Vegas and Grand Canyon

In the same year, Chinnamma and I, along with Chinnamma's brother Appachen and his wife, Leelamma, went to Las Vegas, Nevada. The luxurious hotels, casinos, and shows there were fantastic. The light and water show, and the gondola ride were very interesting. There is no difference in day and night; in fact, the nights there are livelier and more interesting than the days. All together, it is a different world. While there, we also went to see the Grand Canyon. A small plane with four of us and the pilot took off, and we saw the whole Grand Canyon in detail. It is a wonder of God's creation. It is one of the natural wonders of the world. Its natural colors and beauty are beyond explanation.

Hawaii

In addition to our two visits to India in 1998, we were able to visit Hawaii and Florida in the same year. It was my great desire to visit Hawaii. So, we arranged a tour along with Sosamma Mathew, a friend from our church. As soon as we landed at the airport, we liked the native cultural reception. As soon as we came out of Customs, beautiful young girls welcomed us and put flower garlands on us. Then we were taken to our booked hotels. Because it is an island, there are plenty of beaches wherever you look. The shores are lined with hundreds of beautiful four-star and five-star high-rise hotels. In the hotel itself, there were swimming pools and many other amenities. On the shore, there were miles of boardwalk filled with hundreds of people walking, resting, and enjoying the waters and natural greenery. We also went to the world-famous Waikiki Beach. There were thousands of people enjoying the warm water and the vast beach. The tide was high, and we saw several people surfing. It was the first time for me to see that in person.

We had many good experiences in Hawaii. We attended a very interesting Polynesian show. The tickets were expensive, but we could see many cultural programs and dances performed by hundreds of beautiful women and men from the nearby Polynesian islands. This lasted for the whole day, and in between we were provided with Hawaiian food and drinks.

We also visited Pearl Harbor, where there is a war memorial and a replica of the USS *Arizona*, a warship that was attacked and destroyed by the Japanese. We had to take a boat to reach there. While in Hawaii, I was able to accomplish my desire to go paragliding. It was an exhilarating experience. I flew high above the sea, hanging onto a rope attached to a huge balloon. Some people were frightened to look down and see below, far away from the shore. But I liked the adventure and really enjoyed it. I knew Chinnamma didn't want me to do it, so when she was in the hotel room, I went out, giving some excuse, and fulfilled my desire. I only told her after I was done.

Hawaii is very much like my native land, Kerala: lots of greenery, tropical trees, fruits, flowers, and so on. I was very impressed as to how clean and perfect they maintained the whole country. The natives treated us very well. Millions of tourists from all over the world visit that place. When I thought about Kerala, I believed God created it more beautiful than Hawaii, but our people have not bothered to keep it clean or take advantage of the blessings by attracting tourists.

I saw a lot of coconut trees there. But none of them had any coconuts on them. To clear my curiosity, I asked our tour guide why there were no coconuts on the trees. He told me that as soon as the nuts flower, the caretakers climb up and cut them off. The coconuts are not allowed to form. The reason being, if a coconut fell on a tourist, the cost of court cases and rewards would be more than the price they would get from the coconuts. They also cut down any old leaves as soon as they change color from green to yellow. I was amazed at how concerned they were for the welfare of the tourists.

Hawaii consists of five islands. All five islands are tourist centers. It is the fiftieth state in America. We left the capital city of Honolulu and flew to Kona, on the Big Island of Hawaii. It is just half an hour flight. There, we could see live volcanoes flowing from a mountain into the sea below. We hired a small tourist plane for that. From above, we could see the burning red lava flowing into the sea. As it touched the water, we could hear the hissing sound and see the steam. We also felt its heat sitting in the plane flying at low height. We didn't mind the heat; it was a great feeling and experience. Not only that, but I was also able to walk on solid lava, which had cooled down and became solid dry land. Those were all thrilling experiences for me. In addition, we were able to enjoy their local hula celebration, which included local Polynesian songs, dances, and special food. A huge outdoor area is used for this purpose at night, lighted by large torches. The whole program is very attractive and interesting.

London and Puerto Rico

In the middle of this, I was sent to London for a fifteen-day training under the Foreign and Commonwealth Office training service. As I had seen London many times before, I did not bother to see it again. I was also sent to Puerto Rico on official business for five days. Once the official duty was over, I was able to go around and see many interesting places with the help of a tour operator. Puerto Rico is a beautiful tourist center with beautiful beaches and warm weather. It was previously under Spanish occupation, and therefore, the natives speak Spanish and follow much of the Spanish culture. I was able to visit the very old San Juan Fort, a small waterfall, beautiful beaches, and a rainforest.

Alaska Cruise and Pacific Northwest Tour

Alaska is a beautiful place with lots of tourist attractions. So we decided to go there. In 1999, we took a fifteen-day tour of Alaska and the Pacific Northwest, starting from Seattle. Chinnamma and I took a flight from New York to Seattle. As there was a day's stopover there, we went around Seattle and saw its famous underground aquarium. We went underground and walked through a passage. On both sides, there were huge glass walls, divided into many sections. Each section was filled with thousands of gallons of water and hundreds of fishes and sea creatures. As we walked, we felt like we could touch them as they came so close to the glass walls. That was interesting and a new experience for us.

The next morning, we started our tour, taking two luxury buses to Vancouver, Canada. Out of the ninety tourists, we were the only two Indians. All others were Americans. But we all had a loving and friendly journey together. On the way, we were able to see the Cascade Mountains and Mount Saint Helens, a volcano in Washington State. Also, we were surprised to see huge redwood trees in that area. The tree's base was so huge, even ten people standing and holding hands cannot reach the other, and the trees were so high, we couldn't see the tops. That night, we all stayed in a motel.

Next day, we reached Vancouver and boarded a huge ship anchored at the port. We sailed on the ship for the next seven days. We docked at Juneau, Skagway, and Ketchikan. At each place, we took shore excursions. In one of them, we took a narrow-gauge train journey to White Pass summit and saw an old gold mine. Some people were able to pick up some tiny pieces of gold.

While there, we saw totem poles for the first time. The native people called Saxman carve the trees into shapes of animals and humans, painting them different colors. Some trees are huge, over thirty feet high. They were genuinely nice to see. I danced with the natives there in one of their local cultural programs. Those were all interesting times.

The captain of the ship took us to a place called Glacier Bay. We sailed remarkably close to the bay, so we could see the huge ice mountains, which were exceptionally beautiful. Sometimes, portions of a mountain would break off and fall into the water. It was considered good luck if you saw one of those events.

The ship stayed there for a few hours, and hundreds of people went up on the deck and watched, taking photos of the ice mountain. All of them were hoping to see one break off, ready with their cameras. As there was no symptom of any breakage, I earnestly prayed to God to make it possible. After about half an hour, I heard someone say there were signs the ice mountain may break. Everybody waited anxiously, looking to that area. After about another half an hour, a big stone portion fell. After some more waiting, we saw a bigger portion, like a ten-story building, break and fall into the sea. All the people shouted with joy. The ice falling into the water created waves that came high up to the ship. I was incredibly happy and thanked God for fulfilling my desire.

On the Discovery television network, I had seen small seaplanes take off and land on the water. I decided if a chance arose, I would go and fly on one. A tour company called Juneau Ice Field and Glacier Sightseeing operated such a floatplane, and I decided to take a tour at any cost. Initially, Chinnamma was afraid and unwilling to join me. But I persuaded her to come along, and we took off from the water on the floatplane. After flying around for an hour, seeing the icefield and glaciers, we landed back in the water. This was a wonderful experience for me. Ketchikan, Alaska, is known as the Salmon Capital of the World. You get that red-colored fish in abundance there. We had plenty of it in the ship's open grill. The seven-course dinner and the other food available were fantastic.

After the cruise, we returned to Vancouver. After disembarking from the ship, we were led to two buses that took us to see other places in Canada. We saw many places in British Columbia, including the beautiful Cascade Mountains, Okinawan Valley, the peach capital of Canada, and vineyards. On our way back, we visited the biggest hydroelectric power plant in the world at that time, Grand Coulee Dam. It produces 6500 megawatts of power a day.

From there, we passed through the mountain ranges of Montana and Wyoming, Yellowstone, and Grand Teton National Park. After visiting the natural wonders and other beautiful places there, we saw Jackson Hall and waterfalls in Idaho and finally reached Salt Lake City in Utah, where the Mormon Church has its headquarters. We visited the Great Mormon Temple and other interesting places there. On the fifteenth day, we flew back to New York from Salt Lake City. I thank God for the safe journey He gave us.

Singapore and Malaysia

After doing all this travelling, I felt bad because we had not visited any countries in the Far East. Therefore, we decided to visit Singapore and Malaysia on our next trip to India. In 2001, we booked our tickets to India via Singapore and Malaysia, where we could spend a few days. From New York, we traveled by Malaysian Airlines. Their services and amenities were all particularly good. First, we went to Malaysia. I was taken back at the airport itself. Most of the airport officials were young Muslim women. It was a surprise for me to see Muslims working in a public place, after living in India and Qatar for a long time and not seeing a single Muslim lady working in public. The six-lane highways were as good as the American ones, and the five-star hotel we stayed in was very impressive.

We saw the Presidential Palace, which boasted the biggest national flag in the world. We also visited the tallest building in the world at that time, the Petronas Twin Towers. Visitors could not go to the top of the Petronas Tower, but we could climb to the top of the other tower, and we went to the revolving restaurant on the top, where we could see the whole city of Kuala Lumpur. We took a tour of the city and attended a very enjoyable cultural program at night. There were many interesting places, including an international food court. We also visited interesting places and sites in Kuala Lumpur and the city of Penang.

From there, we went to Singapore. Though it is exceedingly a small country, it is very well advanced. We toured the city, went on a river cruise and rail journey, took pleasure rides, and saw the Jurong Birds Park and the Butterfly Park; they were all well-arranged, interesting, and enjoyable. The best thing was visiting Sentosa Island, which we reached by cable car. The whole island is a beautiful tourist attraction. It took an entire day to cover all the attractions and events. There is a statue that's twelve stories high of the state emblem, the Golden Merlion. There were musical fountains, a scented garden, a dolphin lagoon, and other fine attractions. We went to the Singapore Museum, which showed videos of the surrender of Japan after World War II; the life-size wax figures of the American generals and surrendering Japanese officers were very impressive. From Singapore, we went to Kerala, and after spending a few weeks in India, we returned to the US.

In 2002, we returned to Kerala, India. Because there was no one to take care of our big house and properties in Ranny, we sold it to Karimkutty Joy, who was a resident of Ranny itself. But we wanted to have a small place in Kerala, where we could stay when we went on vacation. So, we bought an apartment in Periyar Hermitage, which is between Aluva and Ernakulam, near the Kochi-Nedumbassery Airport.

On our way back, we stayed a week in Doha, Qatar, where we stayed with my nephew Bensey and family. We were also able to visit our old friends and relatives, enjoying their love and hospitality. I was so happy to see the progress and prosperity in that country after just a few years. We also had the privilege to worship and have fellowship with the believers of Ebenezer Brethren Assembly, Doha.

Montreal and Quebec City, Canada

In the same year, we went to see Montreal and Quebec City in the eastern part of Canada. We visited the Montreal Olympic Stadium, underground shopping complexes, and other interesting places. Quebec City is also remarkably interesting. We visited the museum, the port, and other interesting places. It's a French enclave; people there still speak French and maintain the French culture. It is an incredibly beautiful place.

Chicago and Windsor, Canada

In the year 2003, we visited Chicago and spent a few days with the brother of my son-in-law, Tom Benson. Once again, we went around and saw many important places we had not seen before. From there, we drove to Windsor, a small city in Canada, lying across from Detroit. My niece Lizzy and her family live there. There was not much to see there, but we attended a Christian music program that was interesting.

London, Paris, Rome, Switzerland, Holland, and Venice

Also in 2003, we made a tour of a few European countries. The fifteen-day tour covered London, Paris, Rome, Switzerland, Holland, and Venice. It was an exclusive Malayalee group of forty people, consisting of our friends and members of our church, India Gospel Assembly. As Chinnamma and I had already seen London, Paris, and Rome, we did not enjoy those cities. But we took a bus tour through the tunnel below the British Canal, which was something new and interesting.

While in Italy, we also visited the city of Florence, the Leaning Tower of Pisa, and the famous city of Venice. The city standing on water, the canals, and the gondola rides were all new to us. The journey to Switzerland was also remarkably interesting. The snow-covered mountains and the tunnels were pleasing to the eyes. In Switzerland, we visited Geneva, Lake Lucerne, the famous Lion Monument, the UN offices, the showrooms of famous watch companies, and other interesting places.

From there, we went to the city of Cologne, Germany. The Alps Mountains, a miles-long underground tunnel, and Cologne's majestic cathedral were all beautiful and satisfying. From there, we traveled to the old but beautiful city of Amsterdam in Holland. A boat ride through its narrow canals, its famous windmills, and a visit to a cheese factory nearby were all interesting. Millions of people visit all these places every year. As this tour was of exclusive Malayalees and friends, we all enjoyed it very much, as we all could talk and joke in our own language, without any restrictions or fear of offending anybody.

Cozumel (Mexico), Grand Cayman, and Jamaica

Next year, we took a Carnival cruise to Jamaica, Grand Cayman, and Cozumel in Mexico. All those places have tropical climates and look like our native Kerala, with lots of greenery and fruit trees. We went out, took conducted tours, and enjoyed the local people, their culture, and their interesting places. The local tours and the ship journey were all enjoyable.

India: Calcutta, Darjeeling, New Delhi, Jaipur, Jodhpur, and Goa

Though we are from India, we had seen only a few places in the country. Therefore, in 2004, we decided to visit some North Indian states. We booked a fifteen-day tour with the travel agent, who arranged a tour for foreigners mainly from Western countries. So, we got exceptionally good hotels, very good guides, and a car with driver for our local travels. We selected places we had not visited previously: Calcutta in West Bengal, Darjeeling, New Delhi, Jodhpur and Jaipur in Rajasthan, and Goa. Our first flight was to Calcutta. The guide met us at the airport and took us to the hotel. From there, during the next two days, we went to many interesting places like Viceroy House, Ganga River, Howrah Bridge, Jain Temple, and Kali Temple. Also, we were shown the life of the upper class and downtrodden poor class life of people. We were treated with a music festival and special Bengali food. We very much enjoyed the stay there.

Our next visit was to Darjeeling. That also was a special experience. Darjeeling is at a remarkably high altitude. From there, we could see part of the Himalayan Mountain range. It is a specialty there to go out very early in the morning and watch the sunrise. The sight was spectacular. The narrow-gauged train journey through the hills, the world-famous Darjeeling tea estates, and the people's lifestyle in the chilly weather were quite different from other parts of India. We were able to see a Buddhist camp and temple, observed their life routines, and saw a Tibet refugee camp and their handicraft workshop. The hotel there was good, but it took a while to heat up the place. That could be because it was off-season, and there were very few patrons in the hotel at the time.

From there, we flew to New Delhi. Because Chinnamma's cousin and his family lived in Delhi, we did not stay in hotel there. This cousin, Dr. Augustine, is one of the panel members of the president's doctors. Through his influence, we were able to visit the Presidential Palace on our last visit to Delhi. This time, we wanted to visit the Parliament Building. Because of the recent attack on the Parliament House, the security was very tight, and visitors were not allowed. But because of Dr. Augustine's influence, we were allowed to go inside the Parliament Building, escorted by a senior security officer. We even had lunch at the exclusive parliament canteen, as the guest of an under-secretary who was the friend of Dr. Augustine. As we had seen the Taj Mahal and Kuttab Minar earlier, we did not visit those places at this time. But we went to see the beautiful and new Lotus Temple. This temple has a magnificent architecture, and its surroundings are kept in mint condition. Therefore, it is a great tourist attraction.

Jodhpur and Jaipur are beautiful cities. On our way from Delhi to Jodhpur, we were shown a marble cutting operation. Rajasthan marbles are incredibly famous, especially the pink ones. Jaipur is a famous tourist center for foreigners. The palace of the old-time rajas, Hawa Mahal, and other attractions are very popular among foreign tourists. There are over one hundred decorated elephants, and tourists ride them to the palace on top of the hill. We stayed in a palace that was turned into a five-star grand hotel.

In Goa, we stayed in an exceptionally good resort. Several Russian tourists were also staying there. Goa is a naturally beautiful place, like Kerala. Beautiful beaches, plenty of greenery, and their Western lifestyle were all interesting. We were taken to the Saint Thomas Cathedral, where the apostle's body parts are displayed. Goa's nightlife is immensely popular. There are a lot of interesting places in India, and a tourist can easily spend a month here, witnessing the multicultural and multilanguage history of this old country. Make sure you select a good and reputable travel agency.

China: Beijing, Xian, Wuhan, Chongqing, and Shanghai

In 2005, I organized another tour to China. Initially, about thirty people had signed up for it. But later, due to certain inconveniences and sickness, many had to cancel. Finally, sixteen of us were able to travel. Before our visit, we Malayalees did not know much about China. We didn't have a good impression of that country. We thought of it as Communist ruled and very backward. Just because we knew about the Great Wall of China, which is one of the Seven Wonders of the World, and because of a good deal, we decided to visit China. But by the time we finished our tour, our opinion of China was completely changed. The good behavior and discipline of the people, their old culture, and the new development, progress, and prosperity gave us a good impression and a different opinion of the country. Then I thought about our Communist-ruled state of Kerala in India, which is very much against modernization and growth. I think our Communist leaders should visit China and study its tremendous progress, its modernization, and the Western capitalist system China has adopted. I noticed that communism there is used only for discipline, law, and order.

We all enjoyed the arrangements they provided us. We visited five important cities in China: Beijing, Xian, Wuhan, Chongqing, and Shanghai. We also had a five-day river cruise on the Yangtze River. We had to use local flights to go to all major cities. We stayed in five-star or equivalent hotels. From the moment we landed in Beijing, we had an English-speaking national tour guide with us until we departed China. Our luggage was collected from the airport by the tour operators, taken in separate vans, and placed in front of our allotted rooms in the hotels. We rode in a separate luxury tour bus. As soon as we reached the hotel, the tour guide handed over our room keys without any delay. All these things were prearranged by the guide. Our departure from each hotel was handled the same way; by a preset time, we would leave our luggage outside the room.

The porters picked it up and loaded it in the vans. In each city, there was a local English-speaking guide in addition to the national one. We stayed three days in Beijing. We were taken in luxury buses to Tiananmen Square (the largest public square in the world), the Forbidden City, the Temple of Heaven, the Great Wall, and the Royal Garden. We were served terrific food and saw fantastic shows every night at each city. After the first three days, we felt we had already achieved the worth of the tour. Every public place was kept so neat and tidy and in order.

From Beijing, we flew to Xian. That is where the underground Terra Cotta Warriors Museum was uncovered in the year 1974. We were so amazed to witness this museum and the Tang Dynasty Show. From there, we flew to the city of Wuhan. We visited the History Museum and many other interesting places.

From there, we boarded the *Royal Prince* for a five-day cruise on the mighty Yangtze River. The next five days were very enjoyable. We cruised through sky-high gorges on both sides of the river. In addition, one day, we had a side journey through a small river on a small boat, which was unforgettable. We felt so good when the young girl guides on the boat tried to sing Christian songs with us. We were able to tell them about the Gospel of Jesus Christ. We were so happy when we got permission from the officers on the ship for us to have our worship service on a Sunday. They provided us with a private place, bread and wine, and so on. Even some of the crew members watched our worship. We shared the Gospel with some of them. Every night, the crew used to entertain us with very nice shows, dances, and other activities.

We finally reached the town of Chongqing. We saw the beautiful Earling Park. Our ship passed through several large locks, like the Panama Canal. In Chongqing, we saw the largest hydroelectric project and the biggest dam in the world. Tens of thousands of families were relocated from its catchment area. In the same way, I was told that in Beijing, the authorities had to move thousands of people to widen the narrow roads. When we were there, we could see the beautifully maintained six-lane roads in Beijing. We could not see any dust, even on the road or any public places. They were so well kept.

From Chongqing, we flew to Shanghai. There we saw the beautiful Yuan Garden, Jade Buddhist Temple, and the Chaoyang village. We were surprised and amazed at the progress that the city made. It looked like a duplicate of Manhattan. Hundreds of high-rise buildings, shopping complexes, and modern living. What progress. The same night, we were taken to a fantastic Chinese acrobatic show. We were all thrilled to see it.

The next day, we went on a cruise on the Brant Canal and visited a silk factory, a Chinese pottery showroom, and a large industrial estate. The estates were huge and modern. When I asked, the guide told us that during the period of Mao's Communist reign, the people had no jobs, and the ones who had jobs struggled on their meager salaries. But since that policy changed, there's been substantial progress. The United States and other Western countries invested billions of dollars and started huge industries. So millions of people got new jobs with higher salaries. He said the people's standards of living changed, their work ethic improved, and they are very happy now. When I saw these changes, I thought of Kerala; Communist government officials should see these changes themselves and bring those changes in our land for the betterment of our people.

After the tour in Shanghai, we flew back to Beijing and from there took a flight to New York. The Chinese tour was the best and cheapest compared to the other tours we took. There were more than twenty Americans with us, and we had particularly good interactions with them. Probably because of them, the national guide took us to many Western-style and high-class restaurants for lunch and dinner. Altogether, it was a pleasant experience.

Brazil and Argentina

Though we visited many places, we had not gone to South America. So in 2006, we decided to take a tour of Brazil and Argentina. It was a twelve-day tour starting from New York in April. After completing the booking and payment, we began preparing for the tour. I was already dreaming about the places to visit. But when Chinnamma and I went for a regular medical checkup, it was found that she had three blocks in her heart, and one of them was 95 percent in the main artery.

Within the next week, open-heart surgery was performed on Chinnamma. That was in February 2006. With that, the South American tour program became a question mark. Chinnamma asked me several times to cancel it. We paid a lot of money for the tour. If we canceled it, we would lose all that money. I committed everything into the hands of God and prayed for His favor. As the blockage was detected before a heart attack, her heart muscles were not damaged or weakened. And by the grace of God and the special care she received, she had a quick recovery. After the surgery, there were only six weeks before the tour. As I noticed that there were no complications and Chinnamma was recovering well, I took courage and mentioned our tour program to the doctor. He said there was no problem with her heart and no complications connected with the surgery, but if she had the will and courage, she could do it.

It was a long journey with tough tours. According to the schedule, the flight from New York took twenty hours, with a changeover. There were other flights to take, travel on a tour bus, and a lot of walking involved. Still, I encouraged Chinnamma, saying that seeing beautiful places would help her feel better and recover soon. With proper medical treatment and special care from me, she became strong and healthier. Though there was some risk involved, to please me, she agreed to take the tour.

Our flight left JFK New York at 10:00 a.m. and reached Sao Paulo, Brazil, at 9:00 p.m. Then, we had to take a local flight to Rio de Janeiro. Chinnamma was very tired, and it was difficult for her to walk to the other terminal to get to the other plane. She had open-heart surgery only six weeks ago. Anyway, we managed everything and reached our hotel by early morning. It was twenty-four hours since we left home, and I knew it was too much for Chinnamma. I was very particular in giving her medications on time during our journey, and I kept on encouraging her. Above all, the good Lord kept her safe. We were there for five days and saw many important tourist attractions. We were staying in a big hotel right in front of the world-famous Copa Cabana Beach. From the hotel, we just crossed the road, and we were on the beach. Many people spent much of their time on the beach. We felt ashamed to see full families to come to the beach with very little clothing, the tiniest swimsuits and bikinis, exposing much of their body.

Two days later, my cousin Babychayan and Sally, along with some of their friends, came and stayed in our hotel. We were very happy to see them and went on some tours with them. Next day, we went to see Sugarloaf Mountain. We took a cable car to reach the top of the mountain. The sights and views of the natural beauty we saw were hard to explain; it is so beautiful. Similarly, there is another mountain there called Corcovado. That is twenty-four hundred feet above sea level. On top of that, there is a 125-feet-high statue of Christ the Redeemer, which is one of the wonders of the world. We will never forget visiting that statue. Brazil were world champions in football, and it was the birthplace of Pele, a world-famous football player. Football is the main sport of that country. When we were there, I thought I should attend a football game. Luckily, there was a game between two famous teams there, and some of us men went to that game.

It gave me great satisfaction to watch such great world-famous players in action. This stadium was the biggest stadium in the country, although it was not covered. In front of the stadium, the footprints of talented players like Pele, Maradona, and others are imprinted in cement. When visitors stand on them, they achieve a heavenly feeling. I had the privilege to stand on them and feel satisfied.

Then we were taken to a Brazilian gemstone's museum. We enjoyed seeing all kinds of gems and gemstones in nine different spectacular colors. We took a tour of Rio by night and saw a samba show, which were interesting and satisfying. The tour company took us to many other places, including some spectacular churches. After five days in Rio de Janeiro, we flew to see the beautiful Iguazu Waterfalls. We stayed there for two days and saw everything in detail. Iguazu Waterfalls is on the border of Brazil and Argentina. We went to both the Brazil side and the Argentina side and saw very good views. It is not like Niagara Falls or Victoria Falls. Niagara Falls is one huge waterfall, whereas Iguazu is 275 falls spread over two and a half miles. In some places, it was higher than Niagara Falls and wider than Victoria Falls. Iguassu is reportedly better to see than Niagara and Victoria Falls. By seeing it, our hearts, minds, and eyes were fully satisfied. What a natural beauty. It is all the handiwork of our great God. We also went to see one of the largest hydroelectric plants and its high dam, named Itaipú.

Brazil, like India, is a fast-growing and developing country. The people seemed well behaved. Even though they have enough oil for their consumption, many cars have a dual system. Because gas is cheaper than oil, all vehicles run on gas. We could see Paraguay from the border of Brazil. If you pass through a small bridge, you are in Paraguay. We went very close to that border. All these countries have weather conditions like Kerala.

From Iguazu, we flew to Buenos Aires, the capital of Argentina. Bueno Aires is known as the Paris of South America and has many interesting things to see and do. There you can see the widest avenue in the world. It is called the 9 de Julio Avenue. On each side of the boulevard, there are nine lanes of traffic, making it eighteen lanes wide. Also, you can see the world-famous Presidential Palace and its famous balcony, where Eva Peron and other leaders spoke from. I had seen that on television news before, so when I saw it personally, I was delighted.

Its very large cathedral, beautiful Palermo Park, and gardens were all very interesting. There was an open-air grand opera show involving horseback riders depicting the history of Argentina. It was very enjoyable and surprising. Then we took a tour of Buenos Aires by night in a floating casino. It was also interesting and new to us.

On the third day, we took a train ride alongside the Tigre River and then took a boat down the beautiful river itself. Then we took a catamaran to see the Tigre Delta area, which is below sea level and comprises thousands of small islands. That journey and those sites were so beautiful and beyond expression.

Thus, within twelve days, we were able to visit and see many important places and events. We were fully satisfied with the tour. Because we had taken a tour package, the tour guides arranged all the transportation, and they spoke English. For every tour, there would be a large bus full of tourists from different parts of the world. We enjoyed their company also.

Finally, we returned home safely. We thank God for His travel mercies and protection. I specially thanked God for enabling Chinnamma to do all that travelling, without any complications or problems. I also thanked Chinnamma for her courage and cooperation.

India and Thailand

On our vacation to India in 2007, I noticed several advertisements for tours starting from Kerala. One of them was a tour going to Singapore, Malaysia, and Thailand. As we had already seen Malaysia and Singapore, I asked the agent if we could go to Thailand alone. He said it was possible, and we booked with him. There was about forty people from Kerala itself taking the tour of all three countries. It was arranged by Soman's Leisure Tours Company. The owner and manager, Mr. Soman himself, came with us, and it was a well-conducted tour. Soman's also offers tours of Europe and America.

We started from Kochi and flew to Singapore. After a short break at the airport, we flew to Bangkok, the capital of Thailand. During the next four days, we were able to visit many important places and attractions. The Buddhist temple and a huge gold-covered Buddha image were interesting. We saw an ancient temple, and its architecture was amazing. Its workmanship was very beautiful. There are plenty of elephants in Thailand, and they are trained to play games. We saw a soccer game and a basketball game with elephants, which was very interesting. The funniest thing was a boxing match between two orangutans. They are big monkeys but look like short men. There was a boxing ring, and the orangutans had boxing gloves and shoes. And the fight was strictly according to boxing rules. There were several orangutan monkeys among the spectators. When one fellow was beaten down, the winner's side monkeys would clap their hands, laugh, and dance. It was so entertaining, we kept on watching and laughing for a long time.

We also had the opportunity to see many wild animals very close.

The arrangements they made in the zoo were very good. They also had many water sports like boating, scuba diving, and parasailing. I took part in some. I was surprised to see some of our Malayalee ladies taking parasailing. It is also a fact that thousands of people come to Thailand from all over the world for cheap massage and sex tourism.

When we were in Thailand, we had to take a long bus journey for the next destination. Then the tour manager asked everyone to introduce themselves. In our group, there were Hindus, Muslims, and Christians. Everyone took two or three minutes each. When it came to my turn, I said I will need more time to introduce myself and give my testimony or life experience. Everyone agreed to that. I gave a full detail of my life, described my education qualifications, and shared what I have achieved in my life and how my God has blessed me more than my friends, families, and fellow students. I told them that it was all by the grace of God I believed. I said it all happened because I am a child of God, and I also mentioned the glorious hope I have.

Everyone who heard my testimony was very happy, and they all congratulated me. From then on, some people started calling me Sir Mathews, instead of just Mr. Mathews, showing some respect. A few of them asked for my advice on many matters. I realized that God would glorify you if you glorify His name. One in the tour groups was an educational and motivational counselor for youngsters; he encouraged me to write down my life experiences as a book, which could motivate young jobseekers and student who go abroad.

We all left Thailand and reached the next place, Singapore. As they all moved to their hotel, we took our flight back to Kochi. The tour from Kerala was also well organized and enjoyable. As all of us were Malayalees, it had its own enjoyment. If opportunity arises in the future, I want to make use of that facility again. After the return of the group to Kerala, a few people from that group visited me in our flat, including a lawyer and his family and a businessperson and his family.

Edmonton, Calgary, Windsor, Toronto, and Ottawa in Canada

In 2007, we visited many places in Canada. Some places we had already visited, but Edmonton, Calgary, and Ottawa were new to us. We went to Edmonton to attend the wedding of my cousin's daughter. As it was a new place for us, we decided to stay on there a few more days and see everything. They took us to the very large West Edmonton Mall, which has a water park, a wave pool, an artificial beach, and a gallery. It was something new to us, and we enjoyed it.

We also drove up to Calgary and saw the city. When we were in Edmonton, we heard about a huge project that started at Fort McMurray in Alberta, which was about three hundred miles away. It was a process of mining oil sand, which was available in plenty there, just thirty feet below the ground level. In the Arabian Gulf area, they had to dig thousands of feet below earth or sea to find crude oil, whereas in Alberta, oil sand was just thirty feet down. This oil find has made Canada very rich.

I was very interested in seeing this gigantic plant and its operations. So, we took a five-hour bus journey and saw everything and returned the next day. Luckily, my cousin's husband's brother was there to accommodate us and take us around that place, as he worked for that company. It was very exciting to see the gigantic machinery, mining, and oil producing process. If we went a few more miles northward, I was told we could see the wonderful borealis. (This is the northern lights, like in Iceland.)

The visit to Ottawa, the capital of Canada, was also very interesting. As Canada was under British rule, the capital is made up like London. The Parliament House and many other official buildings are very much like British Parliament and other office buildings. Even now, the changing of the guard takes place every day, as it is in London. The guards also look exactly like the Queen's Guards in their uniforms. Thousands of tourists gather every day to watch the changing of the guard, which takes at least half an hour. Ottawa is a very clean and beautifully kept city. We were able to go in and see the Parliament House and other important buildings and monuments. We took a boat ride in the nearby river.

Dominican Republic

In the same year, we went to the Dominican Republic in the Caribbean and spent five days in a large resort there. We went there to escape the chilly winter in New York. The beautiful large pools, saunas, food, beach, and horse rides were all very interesting and enjoyable. We also visited its historic Saint Domingo Port and Rulers Palace, the museum, and so on.

Australia, New Zealand, Tahiti, and Moorea

After all these journeys, I thought I should cover the fifth continent also. So, we booked a twenty-two-day tour covering Australia, New Zealand, Tahiti, and Moorea. Four of our Malayalee friends also joined us. As the tour was starting from Los Angeles, and the flight from Los Angeles to our destination was too long, we decided to leave four days early from New York and spend some time in LA. Though we had visited Los Angeles before, I had two more places in mind to visit and spend some time with our cousins there. So, we visited our cousins there and then settled down with Chinnamma's cousin, Michael Adackapara, and his wife, Rani. Michael was an engineer who worked in the office of California's Governor Arnold Schwarzenegger. According to my interests, we visited the Kodak Theatre, where the Academy Awards are held, Pasadena's Rose Parade area, the Hollywood Hills, and the residences of many famous Hollywood stars. But those four days were very informative and interesting.

At the beginning of the tour, we all gathered at the Los Angeles airport. In addition to the six of us, there were about forty Americans on that tour. We left LA and reached Tahiti, a beautiful island. We had a one-day stopover there, and the next day, we flew into Oakland, the northernmost city of New Zealand. Even though it is not the capital of New Zealand, it is the most populated city and the country's business capital. Our tour started the next day. Everything was arranged by the tour company: our international flights, internal flights, transfer from airports to hotels, and English-speaking guides.

On the first day, they took us to a large museum, to beautiful parks and monuments, and to see native Aborigines and watch some of their dances and other activities. We were also taken to the top of a mountain from where we could see the skyline view of the city and the heart-filling natural beauty. We had a wonderful welcoming dinner in a fantastic restaurant on the top of that mountain. We had to take cable cars to go up the mountain. The first day was extremely exciting and enjoyable. The next day, they took us to some beautiful places and showed us their beautiful houses and their lifestyles, which were also new and interesting to us.

While we were there, my cousin Roy and his wife Glency, and Chinnamma's cousin Dolly and her husband Thomas, visited us in our hotel. That added to our joy. Next day, we took a flight to Queenstown, which is on the south end of New Zealand. That town is situated in between the Southern Alps Mountains and the seashore. Those places are most beautiful to see. The following day, we went on a long drive through a thick forest and reached a big lake called Milford Sound. From there we boarded a ship and sailed for a few hours. The mountains and gorges on both sides, big waterfalls, seals resting on the big rocks, colorful buildings and houses, and the greenery were so beautiful and satisfying to the eyes and mind. We visited other interesting places in Queenstown, and on the next day, we took a special tour bus and went to Christchurch, which is in the middle of New Zealand.

New Zealand is altogether attractive and beautiful to see. Everywhere, you see green-covered land, lots of green trees, hills, valleys, and lakes. It gives a cool feeling to the eyes. When we were in Queensland, we took a tour of the Deer Park safari. There, we could see some rare animals like red deer, bison, and llama. This was the first time we saw some of these animals. In addition, the view from the top of that hill was very attractive. This is the place that was used for the location shooting of *The Lord of the Rings*, *Wolverine*, and the *Rescue* films.

On our way up to Christchurch, we passed Mount Cook and went through many beautiful places. We also passed through the native land of Sir Edmund Hillary, who was the first person to conquer Mount Everest, the tallest mountain in the world. We were told that Sir Edmund practiced mountaineering on Mount Cook. After that, we passed through a village called Fairley. We also spent a day there as a guest of a native New Zealander in a farmhouse. It was a very good experience. Each farmer there had five to ten thousand acres of land and thousands of sheep, cows, and so on. The family we stayed with had four thousand acres of land, five thousand sheep, five hundred cows, and over a hundred deer. They did not milk these animals, but it was for its kids and calves. They were used for its hair and the cows for its meat; companies would come and cut the sheep's wool two or three times a year. This was used for making woolen clothes. To take care of these animals, there were only two or three people, the owner, his wife, and another man. But they had ten to twelve shepherd dogs, which gathered all these animals from this large grassland. We were surprised to see the efficiency of these dogs.

In those places, each house was about twenty miles apart. Even though they are very rich, the people provide lodging and boarding to the tourists who pass through. The tour company compensates them as per previously agreed rates and number of guests. There are no big hotels in that area, but it is a very good experience for the tourists. Six of us stayed in that particular house. Each couple were given a well-furnished bedroom and all other facilities. A whole lamb was roasted for our dinner, and they gave us an incredibly good breakfast also. They were nice loving couple.

Next morning, we left that place and reached Christchurch later that day. On the way, we could see thousands of sheep grazing together, vast vineyards, and very long and sweeping sprinkler systems. We drove for hundreds of miles and did not see any human beings on the way, as people own thousands of acres of land, and the population is very small. People are only in the town areas. Christchurch is very much like a city in England. The Cathedral Square and other sites are remarkably interesting and attractive.

The following day, we flew to the city of Melbourne, Australia. Melbourne is very populated and still growing. We visited many interesting places and enjoyed it, especially the beautiful Fitzroy Gardens, City Square, Victorian Art Center, and the old Parliament House. We also saw Captain Cook's cottage, which is a historical site within the Fitzroy Gardens. Similarly, we saw other interesting places like the Royal Exhibition Building and Saint Patrick's Cathedral; both are very beautiful. Also, we saw the Queen Victoria Market, which has a thousand shops. This place is also a tourist attraction. I was delighted to see the Red Lever Arena (Melbourne Park), which is the home for the Australian Open Tennis Championships.

We all enjoyed an innovative idea, a restaurant on a colonial tramcar. Many tram cars ran across the city, and one was turned into a very good restaurant. From outside, it looked like a regular tram car, but inside, it is a beautifully decorated restaurant. We booked in advance to have dinner on the tram. It is popular with tourists. We started from a particular place, traveled around the city enjoying the sights, and returned to the starting point. During that period, dinner was served, and wine and dessert were also served. While eating, we viewed the attractions of the city through the large glass windows. We enjoyed it very much.

It was another achievement to see the Melbourne Museum and the IMAX Theater attached to it, where we saw *Safari in the Oakarang*, a 3-D African adventure show.

From Melbourne, we traveled to the city of Cairns, which is situated in northeast Australia. That place has tropical climate like our native land Kerala. Lots of fruit trees, vegetables, jungles, and big forests. It has a warmer climate compared to other colder cities in Australia. This is where the world-famous Barrier Reef is situated. This live reef is spread over an area of twenty-three hundred kilometers. This great reef of more than six hundred rocky islands and three hundred coral lakes is one of the wonders of the world. There are four hundred fifty different types of corals, fifteen hundred types of fish, and four thousand types of mollusks. It was my great desire to see this wonder of the world.

According to the prearranged tour program, the next morning, we boarded a high-speed catamaran and sailed for two hours to a small island that was an eco-tourism place. There were beautiful beaches, ponds, guided walking tours, good restaurants, and other amenities. Then we were taken in smaller glass-bottom boats and went over the coral reef and saw different kinds of fish. We went out a few kilometers and returned to the island. Thus, my desire to see this wonder of the world was accomplished. We all enjoyed that visit.

Next day, we went on a ropeway ride called Sky Rail. It was a seven-kilometer-long ride sitting in boxes like gondolas and riding above the thick rainforest. In between, there were a few stopovers towers a hundred feet above the forest. It was so interesting to ride above the treetops. On the way, we could see trees, waterfalls, small rivers, animals, and birds.

From there, we went to Kuntar, an Australian Aborigine village. There, we could see the lifestyle of the original natives, the weapons and tools they used, and the musical instruments they played. We also witnessed some of their cultural programs. This was the first time I ever saw a boomerang. As the word itself means, if we throw this item, it will come back into our hands. But it only comes back to you if you are experienced in throwing it.

The next day, we left Cairns and flew to the most modern and beautiful city of Sydney. Just like Manhattan, Sydney is a big city with lots of high-rise skyscrapers and a large population. One of the modern wonders of the world, the Sydney Opera House is situated there. This building is so beautiful to see. Its architecture, the huge size, and the materials used for its building are wonderful. I consider it as a great privilege that I could go inside and see everything in detail. The huge Harbor Bridge, situated just opposite the Opera House, is also a big attraction. There were provisions to climb to the top of the bridge, but I did not venture to do that, due to the lack of time. Every New Year's Day spectacular fireworks are set off from the top of that bridge. We also had a Captain Cook dinner cruise on a ship in Sydney River. We enjoyed the beautiful night view of the city lights.

Next day, we visited the 260-meter-high Sydney Tower. The view of the city from the top of the tower is spectacular. We also enjoyed watching the 3D *Australian Adventure* show, which was projected onto the tower itself. We also went around and saw the Sydney Olympic Park, the City Center, a shopping center, and an international food court; they were all very good. We very much enjoyed the Botanical Garden and Bondi Beach. We also enjoyed visiting the wildlife park, and we even held a lazy koala in our hands. We can't explain how satisfied and happy we were in our five-star hotel stay in Sydney. We had another privilege to visit and enjoy the hospitality of Chinnamma's cousin Jasmine and her husband, Lijo, who reside in Sydney itself.

From Sydney, we flew to the Polynesian island of Tahiti. As we came out of the plane, beautiful Tahitian girls greeted us with garlands. At the entrance to the airport building from the tarmac, there were four huge native men in their local attire, singing with their local musical instruments. These were all very interesting and attractive to the tourists. We were immediately taken to our resort in an air-conditioned bus. The islands had a tropical climate and were full of green trees, flowers, coconut trees, banana trees, hills, mountains, and water on all sides. It was impossible to explain the natural beauty of the place. There was a large swimming pool and an artificial waterfall alongside it. It was fun playing in that pool. By night, there was a spectacular Polynesian native dance program with sixty beautiful young women and men with their scanty dress of flowers and leaves. The open stage and the colorful lights made it more interesting and enjoyable.

Next day, we took a catamaran to Tahiti's sister island, Moorea. It took us half an hour to sail there. Small planes carried tourists in between these islands. By plane, it takes only seven minutes flight. Moorea is a most beautiful island. Its beaches, hills, and mountains of two thousand to four thousand feet high with lush greenery were very attractive. The island is surrounded with neat and tidy beaches. There are roads circling the whole island. If you take a half-day cycle ride, you can cover the whole island.

We stayed in a five-star resort and spa. On the shores of the whole island, there are hundreds of lagoons. There are also star-rated huts built at the seaside, and some are built out over the sea. The sea there is very shallow and without any tide. Some of them have glass bottoms, so we could see fish and other sea creatures moving under our floor. These huts are more expensive than the hotel rooms. These are very luxuriously furnished and air conditioned. Some of these huts have steps that go down to the water. Hundreds of them are built in an artistic way, and it is very nice to see them. Adjacent to our resort, there was a dolphin center and spa. Because of the pleasant weather and natural beauty, there are always thousands of tourists throughout the year.

From there, we were taken in a boat to a shallow flat place in the sea, where they fed sharks. They had built a stand in the sea from where we could watch the feeding. They announced that the courageous could go into the water and see hundreds of sharks very closely, and you could touch and feed stingrays. I was one among the courageous ones to go in the water and see sharks very closely, and I held many stingrays in my hand. I will never forget that wonderful time.

After staying there for two days, we went back to Tahiti and then left Papeety Airport for the US. Even after such a long tour (twenty-two days), we did not feel tired. Chinnamma had diabetes and many other problems, but even she did not complain. In fact, we did not want to come back from those beautiful places. Our friends who traveled with us were very happy and asked me to decide for the next tour. We thanked God for keeping us healthy and without any problems or accidents throughout our tour Down Under. The three weeks had flown by, and we returned to our home in New York.

Egypt and Jordan

After visiting the Australian continent, we had covered five out of six continents in the world. Then I thought I should cover the sixth one also. That was the African continent. When I considered Africa, Egypt came into mind, as one of the old wonders of the world, the Great Pyramid, is there. In addition, the Petra in Jordan is also considered a wonder of the world. Our friend Idicula Sam and his wife Ponnamma, who came with us to Australia, agreed to join us. So, we chose an eleven-day tour called Pyramids, Nile Cruise, and Petra. There were thirty-four people starting from New York, and we four were the only Malayalees.

We started our tour from JFK on a Royal Jordanian Airlines plane and reached Cairo, Egypt, the next day. The tour operators picked us up and took us to the five-star deluxe Ramses Hilton on the bank of the Nile River. We were amazed at the luxury of the hotel. Afterwards, we were taken to the great Pyramid of Giza, which was more than five thousand years old and was one of the wonders of the world. This was a huge one, and we saw some smaller pyramids also. Then we were taken to see the Sphinx of Giza. The statue is fifty meters long and twenty-two meters high. Its body is the shape of a lion, and the head is that of a tiger. This huge sculpture is carved out of one big rock. Both the pyramids and the sculpture are wonderful. From there, we were taken on a ride of the Cairo City. At night, the view from the hotel room into the decorated Nile River is fantastic.

The next morning, we flew to the city of Aswan. That is where the Aswan Dam is built on river Nile. We took a short tour of Aswan Dam and then took an optional tour to Abu Simbel. There we could see Colossi and Ramses II and a sun temple. They are huge and built on a hill. We all were wonderstruck when we were told that these structures and the hill were removed from its original place, brought here, and reestablished. If it remained in the original place, it would have submerged underwater when the dam was finished. So, they moved everything before the completion of the dam. It was a Herculean effort to move all those stone temple parts and hundreds of stone statues, each weighing more than a hundred tons. It was very exciting to see all that. Then we took a sailboat ride on the Nile River. We also visited Lord Kitchener Botanical Garden, where we had a glimpse of the vast Sahara Desert. That same evening, we boarded a riverboat called M.S. *Tulip* and cruised through the Nile River.

During the next two days, we visited Kom Ombo, Edfu, Esna, and Luxor. We saw many huge temples and the Valley of Kings, where sixty-four pharaohs are buried. Next, we saw the temple of Queen Hatshepsut and the great inner court of Luxor Temple. We were told that the Temple of Karnak took fifteen hundred years to complete. We were surprised and wonderstruck when we saw the huge size and workmanship of these temples. It is beyond anybody's explanation and imagination as to how these large and tall stone pillars and stone slabs were lifted and fixed. At the end of our cruise, we took a flight back to Cairo. There we visited the old city, saw a famous mosque, and went to the Egyptian Museum.

There is very little rain in Egypt. In some places, they get only two or three rains in a year. All their farming, drinking water, and electrical production depends upon the Nile River. The Nile is the longest river in the world. It passes through many other countries before reaching Egypt. God seemed to provide this river for their survival. The Egyptians call it the eternal river of life. We felt very happy and satisfied to go and visit one of the oldest civilizations in the world.

On the evening of the eighth day, we left Cairo and flew to Amman, the capital of Jordan. We spent the night in a hotel in Amman. Next day, we went around the city and then drove to the Rose City of Petra, through the King's Highway. When we reached the city, we had to take a horse carrier and then walk through a very rugged rock cliff to reach the destination. It would surprise anyone to see the building called the Treasury, which is built within a mountain of rock. History says that an Arab tribe called Novatians built it two thousand years ago. *Indiana Jones and the Last Crusade* was filmed here. There are many other rock mountains and large caves built in it, and many people live there. All these rocks are rose color and very nice and beautiful to see.

That night, we stayed in a five-star deluxe resort called Tiamat Zamon Hotel, built on the top of a hill in the fashion of an old Nabataean village. It was a very refreshing experience. From the outside, it looks like very old small mud houses we see in the deserts. But when we get inside, everything is so modern and high-class standard. We were told the resort won many awards for its special architecture and high standards.

Next day, we visited a place called Jerash, which is said to be sixty-five hundred years old. We also visited Mount Nebo, where Moses was buried. From that place, on a clear day, you can see the Jordan River Valley, the Dead Sea, Jericho, and Jerusalem. On our way back, we could also see where the Israelites walked on their sojourn from Egypt to the land of Canaan, and the place where Moses struck the rock for water, Wadi al Moussa. Even now, water is flowing from that place in the desert, which they have preserved by building an enclosure for it.

We were shown the River Yapok, where Jacob crossed the river after wrestling with an angel of God. All these sites and places of biblical history delighted our hearts and eyes. On the eleventh day, we boarded a plane from Amman and flew to New York. We all enjoyed that tour very much. The tour guide and the tour company management were very good.

Aruba, Colombia, Panama, Costa Rica, and Cayman Islands

The months of December and January are very cold in New York, and there are many snowfalls. To escape the severe cold for a few days, we decided to take a cruise ship journey in the warm waters of the Caribbean Islands. So we booked a twelve-day cruise on the Royal Caribbean cruise line. The name of the ship was *Jewel of the Seas*. The ship was twelve stories high with nine passenger elevators, each with a capacity to carry up to twenty people. It had twenty-five hundred passengers and eight hundred sixty staff members. It may be surprising for those who have not taken a cruise to know the details of the ship. This ship was 963 feet long and 106 feet wide. It had its own generator that produced sixty thousand kilowatts of electricity. The daily water consumption on this ship was seven hundred metric tons of fresh water. On the ship, there was a reverse osmosis plant that could produce more than seven hundred metric tons of fresh water from seawater. We took a tour of the kitchen, and I obtained a list of main foods that were used in a week. The list is as below:

18,400 fresh eggs
12,500 pounds of fresh vegetables
11,580 pounds of fresh fruits
31,345 pounds of poultry
7,500 pounds of potato
5,350 pounds of beef
7,500 bottles of liquor
8,500 cans of beer

5,000 cans of soda
4,750 pounds of rice
3,500 pounds of milk
3,650 pounds of sugar
785 gallons of ice cream
556 pounds of coffee

In addition to the breakfast, lunch, and dinner served at large dining areas, food and drinks are available from buffet areas, specialized restaurants, and bars. You can have any amount of food any number of times without any restrictions from the buffet. You must pay at the special restaurants and also at the bar. Similarly, from six o'clock in the morning until midnight, there are so many activities to keep you busy and interested. There are games, shows, a movie theater, a casino, gyms, several swimming pools, hot water whirlpools, water rides, table tennis, shuttlecocks, football, golf, rock climbing, and many other amenities. You can select what you want, participate in it, and enjoy. If you do not want to do any of these things, you can sit or lay down and relax on one of the thousands of beautiful beach chairs or sofas provided on the deck or in the large halls inside the ship. You can also participate in cultural programs that are conducted on board. If you don't enjoy any of that, you can sit in your air-conditioned room and watch TV, read, or sleep.

When we reach port in each island country, we go out and see those places, meet the people, engage in some activities, and do some shopping. While we are on the ship sailing towards the next country, we get details of the available land excursion and other activities. We can book that in advance and pay for it on the ship itself. Then we get reliable operators, and they bring us back to the ship in time before its departure. We can go out and find local operators or taxis at a cheaper rate, but there is always a risk involved in it. Many youngsters prefer to do that, especially if they are in a group.

Our cruise started in Miami. So, we had to fly from New York to Miami; Chinnamma's brother Appachen and his wife Leelamma went with us. It was their first ship journey, and Leelamma was afraid. But once we were on the ship, her fear disappeared, and she started enjoying herself. To board the ship, we had to go through strict security check. As it was a huge ship, we could not feel it shake or move or anything. We all felt as if we were sitting in our home. With so many shops, restaurants, offices, and thirty-five hundred people on it, it looked like a busy city.

Four days after we left Miami, we reached at a small island called Aruba. Though it is small, it is a major tourist center. In all the Caribbean islands, the weather is warm throughout the year, and there is very little rain. So, throughout all the seasons of the year, tourists go there. Main income of the country is from tourism. We had booked a land excursion. So, as we came out of the port, an air-conditioned tourist bus picked us up and showed us around all the important places on the island. The lighthouse and some rocky formations and the beaches were all very interesting. At the end of the day, we were brought back to the ship.

We left Aruba in the evening. After sailing throughout the night, we reached Colombia early in the morning. As we had booked earlier, we took a short tour of Cartagena. Colombia is a big country, and the tour covered one main city only, where we could see the Spanish culture and the historical sites of the Spanish occupation and their rule over there. We could see many forts, dungeons, and the Ruler's Palace and their marketplace. As we landed at each port, there were different kinds of tour packages available to cater everybody's taste and interest, considering our age and health condition. We took tours to see places, people, their culture, and monuments. Every night, after we returned from the land tours, we had dinner on the ship and then saw different kinds of shows, musical concerts, and even magic shows in the ship's large theater. Every day, there were different shows, and all of them were interesting. On top of that, the ladies spent a lot of time in the casino.

We left Colombia and reached Panama on the seventh day. There we took a tour of the Gatton Locks and the Canal Zone. I was very keen to see the world-famous Panama Canal and its operations. I was so glad to go and see all that and learn about the history of the canal's construction. We were also able to travel across the whole width of Panama, traveling from the East End to the West End. From the West

End, we could see the Atlantic Ocean and Pacific Ocean meeting at one place. We were very much impressed of the modern Panama City and its high-rise buildings.

On the eighth day, we reached a place called Puerto Limon in Costa Rica. Costa Rica is very much like Kerala. They too have coconut trees, mango trees, banana trees, jackfruit trees, pineapple, tropical fruits, forests, wild animals, birds, and all kinds of tropical trees and flowers. It is a beautiful place with lots of greenery. I had a chance to have a close look at some birds and animals for the first time. The short train journey we took there through the village was also interesting.

In addition, I went to see a large banana plantation there. It was a well-managed operation. Thousands of plants are planted scientifically. They know that within so many days, it will completely grow, within so many days the bananas will come out, within so many days they will break off the flower part, within so many days they will cut the planters, and so on. Then everything is moved to a processing plant through slow-moving chain lines. Once they reached the plant, they spray pesticides to kill any pests or bugs. Then it will be well washed again and separated by small portions. It is immediately moved into a huge tank full of water. There were many ladies standing there, washing it again, sorting good and bad ones, and filling it into cartons. They are immediately loaded into huge container trucks and moved to the nearby ports for export by ship to America and other countries. It was nice to see this whole process. We had guides to explain it to us. When I saw that, I thought about our beautiful Kerala and the possibility of doing such export-oriented plantations. At the same time, I felt bad that our government and businesses were not taking advantage of such opportunities.

We left Costa Rica and reached the small island of Grand Cayman on the tenth day. Georgetown is the only city on the island. They have a lot of turtle farms there. It is very interesting to visit those farms, which we did. In addition, we took a trolley tour of the city, which took us around and brought us back. There was not much to see there, but they have beautiful beaches and shopping places.

The same night, we left Grand Cayman and returned to Miami

on the twelfth morning. We took a flight from there and reached New York safely.

Because we had the company of Appachen and Leelamma, it was very enjoyable. As it was their first cruise, everything was new to them. But within a day or two, they became accustomed to everything and started enjoying themselves, and we were always together in all our activities. On Captain's Day, everybody dressed in their best and got together to meet and socialize and take photographs with the captain and his deputies. On that day, we all went to dinner in a full suit, and a special treat was given out. In addition, every day, three or four photographers go around and take photos of every event and people in any activity. They take hundreds of photos every day, develop them, and display them on the inner walls of the ship. You can choose a picture and buy it. The price is high, but they make a big business out of it.

On our voyage back from Cayman Islands to Miami, a severe earthquake took place in Haiti. We were just one hundred miles away from the earthquake area. As there was no tsunami, we were not affected by it. God kept us all safe. The next day, the captain initiated a Haiti relief fund, and almost everybody in the ship contributed to it. We are glad that we were also part of that good work.

Appachen and Leelamma were initially hesitant to go on a cruise, but they asked us to arrange one in the next year. We were so happy they enjoyed the tour. As we had a lot of time in Miami before the flight to New York, we took a local tour and visited the Florida Everglades in a hovercraft. It was very interesting, and we could see a lot of birds and wild animals, including alligators.

Russia: Moscow, Uglich, Goritzi, Kizhi Island, St. Petersburg

Russia, which was under Iron Curtain for many years, opened to the world for tourism recently. I had an interest to visit Russia. When I mentioned it to some of my friends, they also showed interest. I got the report that a river cruise from Moscow to Saint Petersburg (formerly Leningrad) was very good and popular. Accordingly, we made a booking in November 2009 to travel in June 2010. If we delayed, we would not get the booking. The demand was very high. Another reason was the ships were smaller in size; they could only accommodate three hundred passengers at a time. There were many such ships. The name of our ship was M. S. *Litvinov*. It was an eleven-day cruise.

There were sixty-two passengers going from New York for this particular cruise. Eight of us were Malayalee. In addition to me and Chinnamma, there were Idicula Sam and Ponnamma Sam, P. V. Simon and Thankamma Simon, and Elsy Mathew and Gracy Mathew.

We boarded the plane at JFK New York, and after a ten-hour flight, we arrived in Moscow. We were received by the ship's agent, who took us straight to the ship. We were welcomed onto the ship by a military band and other welcoming acts. We rested on the ship that night. The next morning, the passengers were loaded onto buses and taken to see many important places in Moscow. Each bus had an English-speaking guide.

Moscow is one of the biggest cities in the world. It has nine million people living in it. We saw the world-famous Red Square, beautiful St. Basil's Cathedral, the Kremlin, the Armory Museum, which contains the Imperial Treasures, and the beautiful Moscow Metro, which is also known as the Underground Palace. We also saw the monuments of Lenin, on one side of the Kremlin. We saw many other important government offices like the KGB, huge Moscow Bell, large and beautiful shopping arcades, and Moscow University. There are also many beautiful artistic churches. They are all very enlightening and heartwarming to see. That night, we saw the fantastic Russian Ballet and a folk-dance program.

Next day, we left Moscow. The ship travelled at night through the Volga River. By next morning, we arrived at a town called Uglich. As we came off the ship, there was a very good welcome reception by beautiful Russian girls. We were taken to the spectacular Cathedral of Transfiguration, Blue Domed Church of Prince Dimitry on the Blood, and other important and interesting places. On that day, we were treated with valuable blini and caviar.

We continued our journey through the river Volga. The next

morning, we reached a small village called Goritzi. There we enjoyed watching the simple village life and some interesting sites. There we also visited White Lake, which is known as the Tisha fishing grounds.

Next day, we reached a place called Kizhi Island. It was a strange and very interesting place. All the buildings were made up of logs; eight-inch and twelve-inch logs were used for walls and ceilings and everything. It is mainly to escape from the extreme cold weather. There were a few churches of beautiful architecture. Some of them had twenty-two big domes built on three stories by wood, without using any nails to join it. It had beautiful, mainly blue colored tiles attached to the outside of the domes, which looked very attractive and wonderful. Then we were taken to a riverside settlement where a lot of their art was displayed. Nearby, there was a large open-air eating place where we were served a barbecue lunch. The arrangement of the tables and chairs itself was very attractive and could accommodate more than three hundred people at a time.

Next day, we reached the city of Saint Petersburg. Saint Petersburg is a very beautiful place. The large European-style buildings and the luxury within are spectacular. In Saint Petersburg, I saw the largest single building, spread over a kilometer. The beautiful and spectacular palace, park, and fountains named after Peter the Great were beyond explanation. Everything looked like real gold. It soothes the eye, heart, and the liver.

Similarly, the Catherine Palace, which was previously known as Pushkin, is also worth seeing. It was very well maintained. Before entering, you must cover your shoes with a special disposable cover supplied to every visitor. You are not allowed to step on its floor with your bare shoes; they have arranged shoe covers for thousands of tourists who visit that place every day. We also saw the Royal Palace, where foreign rulers and dignitaries meet, and where meetings are held by Russian presidents and other visiting state officials. The City of Canals and Saint Isaac's Cathedral were also very interesting and beautiful.

Next, we visited the Hermitage Museum. The Crown Jewels, paintings, statues, and architecture are world famous. We were all fully satisfied by visiting that museum. We saw many churches and cathedrals in that Communist country, so I asked our guide if there were any Christians there. The answer surprised all of us. She said that 98 percent of the people are Russian Orthodox Christians. She also told us that for seventy-five years, the Communists tried to improve the condition of the people, but the result was severe poverty. She also said that now there is much progress as the power of communism is reduced.

Thus, after a very enjoyable and satisfying Russian tour, we returned to New York on the twelfth day. Our friends who joined us also enjoyed it very much, and they thanked me for arranging it. Thank God for His care and protection throughout our journey.

CHAPTER 9

Addendum

All that you have read so far is a revision of a book I wrote in Malayalam and published in India, mainly for our family, friends, and church members. It contains events and experiences until early 2010. Since then, ten more years have gone by, and a lot of new events have taken place.

I would like to mention a few of them, as I continue to enjoy the grace of God.

In 2011, we went to Dallas, Houston, and San Antonio. While in Dallas, we revisited the place where President John F. Kennedy was assassinated. In Houston, we visited a few friends and families. Then we went to San Antonio, where a cousin of Chinnamma, Biju and Sini, were staying. We stayed with them about four days and went around and saw a lot of beautiful places. San Antonio is a wonderful city for sightseeing. There we walked through a scenic river walk, dined at specialty restaurants, and took a river cruise along the San Antonio River, flowing through the city center. We visited the Alamo mission center, one of the most important historical sites in the US. We also visited the 750-foot-tall Tower of America. We had a panoramic view of the whole city of San Antonio from the top of the tower. We also visited the San Antonio Botanical Garden. While in San Antonio, we had the privilege of visiting the headquarters of firebrand evangelist John Hagee.

Same year, we went to India and stayed there nearly five months. During that period, we took a tour to Hyderabad and Secunderabad. We took a flight from Cochin to Hyderabad. From the airport to the hotel, we passed through the longest flyover, to my knowledge, in India at that time. I think it was more than twelve miles. I was impressed with that. In Hyderabad, we saw almost all the important places like Charminar Mosque, Golconda Fort, Salazar Jung Museum, a Buddha statue in the middle of a heart-shaped lake in Hussain Sagar, Ramoji (a film city), Chowmahalla Palace, Mecca Masjid, Birla Mandir, Qutb Shahi Tombs of Dynasty Rulers, and an artificial snow city. All these were very interesting and impressive sights to see. The Ramoji Film City was a special experience for me. We also had the privilege to dine on the special and classic Hyderabadi biryani. We also took a tour of the fast-developing industrial estates in Hyderabad. While there, we also visited the nearby city of Secunderabad.

Next year, we had to attend a wedding in Atlanta. While there, we visited a few friends and the city of Atlanta and the Coca-Cola Center. We had Chinnamma's nephew, Saji, with us.

After the wedding, we took a tour of the nearby state of Tennessee and the famous music city of Nashville. Nashville is a vibrating city with a big music industry. We walked around all those famous city streets and visited the art museums and the Grand Old Opry. We visited the Country Music Hall of Fame and Museum. We visited the Parthenon, a replica of the original Parthenon in Athens, and a forty-two-foot-tall statue of Athena. We took the General Jackson showboat dinner cruise on a paddlewheel boat, sailing through the beautiful places of interest on the sides.

In Tennessee, we also saw Chattanooga and beautiful Lookout Mountain, from where you could see four nearby states. We also saw Ruby Falls, the largest waterfall in the US and adjoining deepest cavern in the US. The cave journey was a real-life experience. We also visited the Lost Sea Adventure.

That same year, in October 2011, we visited India and stayed until March 9, 2012. While in India, I had the opportunity to do many door-to-door house visits along with a dozen evangelists and proclaim the glorious Gospel of Jesus Christ and distribute hundreds of tracts and Bible portions. By the grace of God, we were able to lead a few people to salvation. During the vacation, I had the privilege to sponsor a small house to a poor family. One man of God donated nearly half an acre of land, and five people sponsored five houses for the poor.

In 2012, we booked a tour of South Africa, but it was cancelled due to Hurricane Sandy.

So, at the end of 2012, we went to India again and stayed there from November 2012 to March 2013. While in Kerala, I was able to participate in many Gospel works and house visits. On our return journey, we stopped over in Doha, Qatar, and stayed there for a week. My nephew and his family lived there, and we stayed with them and visited several of my cousins, old friends, and the Doha church members. I had the privilege to attend the new church complex and give my testimony and minister the Word of God in Ebenezer Brethren Assembly. We were able to enjoy the love and lavish hospitality of our family, friends, and relatives there.

We were surprised and very happy to see the progress Qatar had made. Doha had become a most modern city, with beautiful high-rise buildings, hotels, businesses, and roads; the city had a much higher population than when we left Doha in 1983. There have been vast developments in industry, farming, tourism, air travel, sports, and so on. The changes were so big that we could not even recognize some of our most familiar places. We visited several places and had a wonderful time there. We were glad to see that the government had allowed freedom to build churches and conduct open worship without fear. Thank God for working in the mind of the ruler. By end of March, we were back in New York.

In June 2013, we had to make a two-week visit to Bombay for the funeral of my sister, Annamma Mathew, who passed away. Later in the same year, we went back to India and stayed there for five months, from October 2013 to March 2014. During this time, I was able to make several door-to-door house visits with a dozen evangelists and spread the Gospel among Hindus, Muslims, and nominal Christians. It was also a pleasure to lend a supporting hand to a number of evangelists in Kerala.

On our way back, as we had planned earlier, we stopped over in Dubai for a few days. Though we had visited Dubai earlier, we were keen to see the newly opened tallest building in the world, Burj

Khalifa. On our previous visit to Dubai, we also visited Abu Dhabi and Sharjah. At that time, we were able to have coffee and snacks from the restaurant of the one and only seven-star hotel in the world, the beautiful Burj al Arab, built on a man-made island in Dubai.

This time, we went up to the top of the world's tallest building, Burj Khalifa, and saw the nearby complexes, including a huge aquarium inside a shopping complex. I was amazed at the number of high-rise buildings and the palm island they created in Dubai. We were also amazed to see our tourist bus, after driving through the city, riding straight into a canal and sailing like a boat in water, for an hour or so showing many waterside sites and buildings. This was my first experience of a regular bus running on land and sailing in water also. We had our cousins, Saji and Reji, and their families to take care of us. Then we returned to the US.

In July 2014, we had the privilege of attending the Annual Gideon's International Convention in Philadelphia. It was a great event, attended by more than three thousand Gideons and auxiliary members from all over the world. Great men of God spoke from the Word of God, and many gave inspiring testimonies. All of us had a wonderful time of friendship and fellowship. We also took a tour of the oldest Bible printing press in the US. It was very interesting to see different process and stages of millions of Bibles being printed, sorted according to different languages, stored, and dispatched to hundreds of countries all over the world.

In the same year in September, we went on a tour of the treasures of Turkey. It was a fourteen-day tour covering Istanbul, Ankara, Cappadocia, Antalya, Pamuk Kale, Izmir, Ephesus, Canakala, and Troy.

Turkey is a beautiful country that millions of tourists visit every year. It is the meeting place of East and West. It has thousands of years of history, an early Christian era, the Roman ruling, and the Muslim era. The old trade route from Asia passes through Turkey, and we saw a model of a caravan resting place and horse lyre.

Though Ankara is the capital, Istanbul is the main business and cultural center. It is a very modern city with lots of historical monuments, as it was called the cradle of civilization.

In Istanbul, we saw the famous Blue Mosque and Sultanahmet Square. We also visited the Gaia Sofia Museum, which was previously a church for 916 years, a mosque for 481 years, and a museum for the last seventy-plus years. You'd be surprised to see the huge structures built more than fifteen hundred years ago in the early days of Christianity. We also saw the spice market and the grand bazaar, where millions of different objects are sold through thousands of shops in a huge, covered building. We also visited the Yerbatan Cistern, which is a wonder. These are huge underground water storage places that store up to eighty thousand square meters of water, and its depth is eight meters with a surface area of about ten thousand square meters. We were told there are more than fifty such cisterns in Istanbul built during the Byzantine period. We also visited the Byzantine Basilica.

We took a boat ride through the Sea of Marmora that took us under the Bosporus Bridge that connects the European continent and the Asian continent. On the way, we saw many great mansions on both sides of the narrow strait. We had a short visit to the capital, Ankara, and then traveled through the beautiful Konya to reach Antalya, where we explored the architectural wonders there and enjoyed the turquoise coast.

We visited the Pamukkale Hot Springs and the "cotton castle," formed by snow-white limestone into travertine terraces. These are natural wonders and beautiful to see. We saw the destroyed ancient city of Hierapolis also. It was an experience to walk through the old ruins.

In Cappadocia, we visited the rock city, where the rocks are carved into rooms, which were a sanctuary for the persecuted Christians in those days. I was able to climb into one large room where they worshipped and broke bread. We could see a stone table. When I say a large room, it may be eight by six by five feet dug in the rock.

Then we moved on to Izmir and went an excursion to Ephesus. We had a detailed tour of Ephesus. I couldn't find the Ephesus church there or any of the other seven churches mentioned in the book of Revelations, which were in the nearby vicinity. They were all destroyed. But there were remains of so many other major structures that were ruined during many occupations. The temple of Artemis was one of the glorious temples. The town planning, the huge structures, stadiums, road works, and so on, built in the first century or even before Christ, are very impressive and had good engineering. And in Ephesus, we also saw the house of Virgin Mary. We also saw Kaymakali, an underground city, and a carpet-weaving center in the city of Pergamum. Then we visited the legendary city of Canakkale and Troy, which is the subject of Homer's *Iliad*.

At Cappadocia, we had the opportunity to witness a performance by the whirling Dervishes. Several men dressed in white spin in perfect harmony. It is part of the Turkish culture. It was interesting to see that. There is much more to write about this tour, but I do not want to go into detail. All together, the tour was very interesting, educational, and enjoyable.

The same year in November, we went to India and stayed there until the middle of March 2015. During that period, I was able to take part in a Gospel outreach training program in Vellora, Kannur, a Communist fort, and distribute tracts along with the students of Pathanamthitta Bible School and encourage them and the believers in Vellora Assembly by giving my testimony and financial help to the poor and needy.

I also had an opportunity to visit the students of Vedanadam Bible Institute in Angamaly and encourage them by giving my testimony and providing financial help for the students. I also enjoyed visiting the Aluva Sub Jail, along with the brethren in Aluva Brethren Assembly, and proclaiming the Gospel to the prisoners and giving them cake and singing Hindi songs to the Hindi-speaking prisoners. During our door-to-door Gospel work in Ernakulam district, along with a dozen evangelists and members of the Aluva Brethren Assembly, I was able to lead two people to the Lord by the grace of God.

It was also a matter of great joy to share the Gospel to several people at a naturopathy center in Kakkanad, where Chinnamma and I were taking treatment for two weeks. I hope it bore fruit, as two people were taking a keen interest in listening and asking questions.

A Turning Point in My Life

By the middle of March 2015, Chinnamma and I were back in New York after four months' vacation in India. Everything was going well, until one day in the middle of April, Chinnamma complained of severe stomach pain. I wanted to call the emergency, but Chinnamma prevented me, saying it could just be gas. I gave her some antacid tablets, and she felt better. Suddenly, she felt severe pain again but did not want me to call 911. So, I said I would take her to the nearby hospital for a checkup. She agreed, and we started off for the hospital, when she started vomiting. She vomited so much, it covered all the front seat of my car, and she slumped over. I stopped the car and tried to help her, so she won't choke on her vomit. She vomited again, and I was also covered in her vomit. Trying not to panic, I ran to a nearby shop and got some paper napkins to wipe her face. I tried to help her sit up and then called 911, but there was no response. So, I continued to drive to the hospital, which was less than a mile away.

We reached the hospital, and they immediately took her to the emergency department. They gave her necessary care and treatment, and she felt better. They found out that her upper hernia was inflamed and suggested removing it immediately. A similar bout had occurred when we were in India, and the doctors there told us to attend to it when we got back to America. So, we talked it over and decided to have it removed. But in the middle of the night, they arranged the surgery in a rush, and it was done in the early hours of the next day. It was done at Saint Joseph's Hospital in Bethpage, Long Island, New York.

For the first two or three days, Chinnamma felt better. The pain was gone, even though the effect of the anesthesia had worn off. She started smiling, and that evening, before I left her, we prayed together. I made her pray to make sure she was in her proper senses. She did it well, and I went home.

Early the next morning, I received a call from the doctor saying Chinnamma was in critical condition and I should get to the hospital immediately. I drove to the hospital along with my daughter Jean and her husband. We informed our second daughter, Judy, and her husband, Sunny, and they arrived at the hospital a little later.

We were told that Chinnamma's wound had become septic, and she had septicemia. Therefore, they pumped in a lot of water into her body, hoping to clear the poison, and she looked double her size. Her kidney was not functioning well, and due to the flooding of the lungs, they were also not working. They kept her there for two days and then transferred her to North Shore University Hospital in Manhasset, which was about twenty-five miles away from our home. Chinnamma was miserable and in critical condition, and we were very concerned about it. But all we could do was to pray and depend upon the expertise of the doctors.

Chinnamma was in the ICU for more than two months. For the first month, she was unconscious, and all we could do was to look at her and pray for a miracle. Then, I believe, God worked, and she became conscious. But she had lost much of her memory and didn't even recognize us. Her wounds were all opened and wouldn't heal, due to her chronic diabetes. Those were the worst seventy days in my life; I almost broke down. Every day, I had to drive a hundred miles going and coming home, twice a day, and sitting in front of a serious ICU patient was a horrible thing. All I could do was pray; my family and church members supported me through their prayers and personal visits and kind words, for which I am very grateful.

As I drove my car to the hospital, in desperation, I used to sing loudly, "The Lord is good, my Lord is good, He has proven to me He is good, everyone on earth ought to know it that Christ the Lord is good." A few months later, I completed it as a Christian song and later recorded it for the glory of God.

As the full coverage of the insurance was about to end, one day, I was told Chinnamma had developed pneumonia, and she passed away within twenty-four hours. After they warned us, we were able to alert all our immediate family and church members, and many came to be at her bedside at her last moment of life. On July 9, 2015, in the presence of family, friends, and church members, and while Brother Daniel Varghese said prayers, Chinnamma closed her eyes and joined her eternal Father in heaven.

Chinnamma's memorial and funeral services were conducted in a fitting manner on July 16 and 17, 2015, under the leadership of India

Gospel Assembly's Elder, Brother Daniel Varghese. As a provision of God, our dear brother John Kurian, prominent evangelist and convention speaker from India, was in the US at that time, and he ministered the Word. Chinnamma's body was buried in Pinelawn Memorial Park and Garden Mausoleum, in Farmingdale, New York, for resurrection at the Second Coming of our Lord and Savior, Jesus Christ.

Some friends advised me to file a case against the hospital for Chinnamma's untimely death. But as I believe that nothing happens without the knowledge and approval of our loving God, and to maintain my Christian ethics, I did not file a case against the doctors or the hospital.

It is difficult to live without my loving wife of forty-seven years. But my loving God has given me His good friendship and company, and He gave me good health to manage my affairs, and I am happily living with Jean and Tom. Since I do not have to worry about my sick wife anymore, I decided to spend more time and money for the service of God and for the Gospel work.

Living Alone

I decided to spend six months in Kerala, India, so I could visit more family and friends, and devote more time for Gospel work. So, I left New York by the end of August 2015 and didn't return until the end of February 2016. While there, Brother Jojo P. J., evangelist of Aluva Brethren Assembly, and I visited Brother T. J. Thomas and family at Bilaspur in Chhattisgarh, North India. While there, I was able to give my testimony and do the Word ministry in the local Hindi Assembly and visit the home of the evangelist there. In addition to visiting some other brethren there, we also visited a coal mine in Korba, which was a new experience for me. Brother T. J. Thomas is an elder in the local assembly and a Gideon like me. He and his wife Elsy made our stay with them very interesting and comfortable.

In September 2015, Jean and Tom came to Kerala, and they had a housewarming for their new house they built on seafront property in Varkala, Kerala. I stayed with them for a few days and enjoyed the beautiful surroundings.

Later, I visited most of my extended family and friends; many of them are old and sick, and they could not afford to visit me in New York. So, I visited them, and it was a very happy occasion for them and me, as well.

In October 2015, I attended a one-week Shepherds Training and Counseling Seminar arranged by Brother Alexander Kurian and Brother John Kurian at the Rehoboth Theological Institute, in Thrissur, Kerala. It was a blessed occasion, and I met many great men of God and had fellowship with them. I also had the privilege to meet Miss P. N. Tressure, custodian of Rehoboth Orphanage in Thrissur, and give them a contribution. I also was able to attend the 110th anniversary of Rehoboth Orphanage in December 2015.

In February 2016, I was able to assist an evangelist and his family, who came from Rajasthan, North India for their daughter's wedding. They didn't know anyone in Aluva, and they were staying in a hotel until I brought them to my apartment and gave them all necessary help. They were with me for a few days and went away happily after conducting their daughter's wedding. They were Evangelist V. M. George, his wife, daughter Joyce, and son Sam.

In August 2016, I turned seventy-seven. Over the next five years, I traveled extensively, visiting friends and relatives, attending weddings, funerals, and family gatherings in New Jersey, Connecticut, Philadelphia and the Poconos in Pennsylvania, Chicago, Indiana, Maryland, Dallas, Houston, Austin, and Orlando in the US and Windsor, Toronto, Mississauga, Hamilton, and Vancouver in Canada. In addition, I visited Cancun in Mexico and took a cruise to Cozumel along with my younger sister, Kunjumol, and her husband, Raju. That was a very interesting and memorable event. Over the next four years, I visited India five times.

I also took several tour packages covering Cape Town, Pretoria, Durbin, Johannesburg, and Kruger Land National Wildlife Safari in South Africa. Also, I visited Zululand in Swaziland, Victoria Falls in Zimbabwe, and Safari Park in Botswana. I also visited Tokyo, Osaka, Kobe, Mount Fiji, Hiroshima, and a Toyota car factory in Japan. In addition, I visited Vienna in Austria, Prague in Czech Republic, Budapest in Hungary, and Bratislava in Slovakia, all in

Central Europe. Though these were all very interesting and exciting journeys, I'd rather not take the pages to give those details.

The COVID-19 pandemic stopped me from going to India in 2020 and 2021 and delayed my visit to Spain and Portugal in 2020. However, I was able to do a fifteen-day tour from September to October 2021, along with my niece Jainamma, her husband Babukutty, and Chinnamma's nephew Saji. I don't want to give any details of those tours either, as it may bore some people. But I will just mention the beautiful places I visited in those two countries just for your information and to encourage travelers like me. I was glad to meet some other extensive travelers during this trip and share their experiences.

In Portugal, we visited Lisbon City and Sintra, the "glorious Eden" of Lord Byron, and the summer retreat of the kings, the Royal Court, the Royal Palace, and so on. Then we moved on to Spain. We visited many interesting and beautiful places in Spain. We toured Seville, Cordoba, Costa de Sol, Rhonda, and Malaga. From there, we visited the famous Rock of Gibraltar, which is a British possession. Then we continued our tour in Spain, visiting the Moorish-influenced Alhambra, Granada, and Toledo. Then we toured the capital city of Madrid and nearby Escorial. Then we took a high-speed bullet train to Barcelona. This is Spain's second-most important city with several museums, galleries, the Olympic complex, Plaza de Catalunya, and the colossal and iconic symbol of Barcelona, La Sagrada Famillia Church, which has been under construction for the last hundred years and still unfinished. Our final visit was to the wonderful mountaintop of Montserrat and the Royal Basilica there. It would take days to describe the beauty of that place and the fantastic work that has been accomplished there, hundreds of years ago. All these journeys and my accomplishments are nothing but the abundant grace of God. All praise and glory to Him. I also want to mention that all the tours I took were guided tours with a group of people. Wherever we go, we would have English-speaking guides, and therefore not knowing a foreign language was not a problem. Not only that, our air travel, local travel and transportation, first class accommodations, and most meals were provided by the tour operators.

In addition to the above, we used to attend the Indian Brethren Fellowship (IBF) Conferences starting from 1992 to 2019, held in Virginia, Ohio, and Indiana. Also, we used to attend FIBA conferences almost every year from its inception in 2004. These were held in different cities and states like Houston, Atlanta, Philadelphia, Dallas, Chicago, and Orlando in the US and Hamilton and Toronto in Canada. Those were all great times of spiritual edification and sweet fellowship.

I want to mention a few things I did while in India proclaiming the glorious Gospel of Jesus Christ and promoting Gospel workers, the evangelists working in a difficult field. In December 2016, I went to Madurai, accompanied by Evangelist Jojo P. J. of Aluva Brethren Assembly, to the place where Evangelist M. E. Cherian created the Madurai Bible School and *Suviseshakan* magazine. I also visited the first Assembly Hall he started in Madurai and his burial place. I met with his sons James Cherian and Johnson Cherian and some students and staff of Bible School and *Suviseshakan*. We arranged a one-day seminar for more than forty evangelists and their families in the surrounding area. I had the privilege to give my testimony, ministered the Word, and provided financial support to the evangelists. Food was also provided to all. That was a blessed time of Christian fellowship and friendship, and everybody liked and enjoyed it. On our way back, we were able to fellowship with Evangelist S. Stephen and worship the Lord at the Theni Assembly. Brother Jojo drove all the way to Madurai and back, and we thanked God for giving us a safe journey.

In 2017, I arranged a one-day program for more than fifty evangelists and their families from Kazargod and Kannur districts, where I delivered my testimony and my Word ministry. Food and financial assistance were provided to all of them to encourage in their work. That too was a blessed occasion.

Also in 2017, I visited Saint Thomas Mount in Chennai. That is the place where Apostle Thomas was said to have been shot by his Brahmin assailant with a bow and arrow. I also visited the well-known

Preacher R. Krishnakutty at his residence in Thiruvattar, where he was bedridden due to a serious illness. In the same year, I had to make a second visit to Bombay because my second sister, Saramma, passed away and went to her eternal home with the Lord.

The same year, we arranged a one-day seminar for the evangelists and their families of Waynad, Calicut, and Malapuram districts. There were over 120 members in attendance. It was held in Calicut City Brethren Assembly Hall, where a few their elders and others lent me a helping hand. I also gave my testimony and Word ministry, and many were encouraged by it. Food was provided to all, and financial assistance given to all the evangelists.

In 2018, we arranged a gathering of more than a dozen evangelists from Ernakulam District, with whom we make home visits and distribute tracts. Food and financial support were provided to all of them. In the great flood of 2018 in Kerala, many people lost their houses and property. I was able to help a brother to rebuild his house. I also visited the first Bible Museum in India, which is at Vempayam, in Trivandrum, Kerala State. It is quite impressive. I don't think many people know about it. It is worth visiting; I hope more people learn about it and visit the museum. It was also interesting to visit the world's biggest bird sculpture, Jatayu Adventure Centre, in Kollam, Kerala.

In 2018, my younger brother-in-law, Scaria Adackapara, passed away, and I went to Kodencherry, Kerala, to participate in his funeral service. I also attended a few weddings of my cousins and others during that vacation.

On my trip to India in 2019, I was able to visit Pathamithitta Bible Institute and make a contribution for a new library being constructed. It was also a blessing to attend the Pathamithitta Brethren General Convention of 2019.

In January 2020, a one-day seminar was arranged for the evangelists in Palakkad district and their families, along with their monthly meetings at Erikum Chira Brethren Assembly Hall, where more than two hundred believers were assembled. I was able to give my testimony, and Evangelist Jojo P. J. gave the message. It was a nice time to see some dear ones like George Peter of Chittoor and other servants of God. Food was provided to all, and all the evangelists were given financial support to encourage them.

I am not writing all this for my fame but to educate and encourage the young generation and the retired community. Those who are young are especially in a far better condition than me, and if they are willing, they could do a lot for the furtherance of His Kingdom in these end days. May God help you all.

As time passed, I was elected as the vice president of the Gideons Nassau Camp. I was also blessed with the position of president and elder of India Gospel Assembly. None of these are because of my merits, but the grace of God, for which I am thankful to the Lord. May His name be glorified through me.

CHAPTER 10

In Short

I was an Indian citizen with an educational qualification of secondary
school certificate; I worked in the Foreign and Commonwealth
Office of the British government for thirty years. I joined them as
a court clerk in Doha, Qatar, and retired as accountant and head
of the Accounts Department in New York. During this period, I
worked in close contact with ten British ambassadors and five British
consuls general. In a diplomatic office where the highest standard
of work, ethics, and discipline is maintained, I was able to achieve
four promotions, whereas many British nationals who worked with
me for long periods of time were not promoted. I am also proud and
happy to mention that a certificate praising my faithful service and
appreciating the contributions I made to the British government was
prepared and signed by the foreign minister, Honorable Robin Cook
himself, who sent it from London to New York in a diplomatic bag
to be presented to me at my farewell party.

- The *British Diplomatic List* is a quarterly published magazine
  that records the names of top British diplomats and officials
  of every post. But the name of this SSLC-qualified Indian
  was also included in the magazine and distributed to all the
  diplomatic posts all over the world for five years. I consider
  it as a big credit for me.
- Normally, only diplomats from the UK are given check-
  signing authority. But in my case, a special authority was
  obtained from the Treasury Department in London, giving

me check-signing authority, and I signed thousands of checks for the British government. One of them was for $80 million (of course, there was always a second signature of the management officer or another diplomat from London). As far as I am concerned, it shows the trust they had in me. It was a great thing to be faithful in whatever is entrusted to us.

- I had the privilege to personally meet and shake hands with Her Majesty Queen Elizabeth and her husband Prince Phillip of the United Kingdom. Not only that, but I also personally saw British Prime Minister Margaret Thatcher, John Major, and Foreign Ministers Sir Douglas Hurd, Malcolm Rifkind, and Robin Cook.

- It is another matter of pride for me that when we were in Doha, Qatar, the British ambassador, the Lebanese ambassador, the Indian charge d'affaires, and some other diplomats attended a party that was arranged in our house.

- I was also pleased to attend the fortieth anniversary of the UN General Assembly, along with more than 160 world leaders and heads of states like presidents, prime ministers, and kings from all over the world.

- I also had the privilege to see in person Pandit Jawaharlal Nehru, Indira Gandhi, and Rajiv Gandhi, prime ministers of India.

- I was lucky to see personally US Presidents Ronald Reagan, George Bush Sr., and Bill Clinton. I also saw Secretary of State Henry Kissinger, Hillary Clinton, and New York Governor Mario Cuomo.

- I also saw personally Russian Foreign Minister Eduard Shevardnadze and Australian Prime Minister John Howard.

- It was very satisfying to meet and shake hands with the former world heavyweight champion Muhammad Ali and his wife Veronica. I've met top sports stars like Tiger Woods, Roger Federer, Rafael Nadal, Steffi Graf, Serena Williams, and so many other world champions. I personally attended baseball, basketball, badminton, boxing, cricket, wrestling, football, ice hockey, soccer, tennis, golf, and horse races in the US, England, India, and Brazil.

- I attended the crusades of Pope John Paul, Billy Graham, and Jimmy Swaggart and personally watched the New York Marathon, ten thousand people tap dancing at a festival, July 4th fireworks, St. Patrick's Day Parade, and so on.

- I have seen six of out of the seven wonders of the ancient world: the Great Wall of China, Petra in Jordan, Christ the Redeemer in Brazil, Chichen Itza in Mexico, the Coliseum in Rome, Taj Mahal in India, and the Great Pyramid of Giza in Egypt. The seventh one is Machu Picchu in Peru, which I have not yet seen.

- Similarly, there are seven wonders of the modern world. They are the Channel Tunnel between England and France, CN Tower in Toronto, Empire State Building in New York, Golden Gate Bridge in San Francisco, Itaipu Dam in Brazil, and the Panama Canal. The seventh one is the delta works in Netherlands. I have visited all these, except the delta works in Netherlands.

- I have visited more than five hundred tourist attractions, spread over fifty countries covering all six continents. I also visited forty out of the fifty states in the US, eight out of ten provinces in Canada, and fifteen out of twenty-eight states in India.

- I purchased and distributed thousands of New Testament Bibles all over the world through the Gideons international and the American Bible Society. I also witnessed and proclaimed the Gospel to many and led more than thirty to salvation, with the help of the Holy Spirit.

- Even though I am not much educated, God has enabled me to write lyrics to over fifty Christian songs. One is in Hindi, half a dozen are in English, and the rest are in Malayalam. Many of them have been recorded in three CDs, and a few of them have become very popular in proclaiming the Gospel. Also, I have written many poems based on biblical subjects that are made into two books. In addition, I have written and published my own autobiography in Malayalam, which has encouraged many Bible school students. I have also received an award from the Bible Literature Forum in Houston, for my outstanding contribution of poems to Christian literature. This also is achieved by the grace of God. Also, God enables me to take Bible studies, Word ministries, and other spiritual ministries as and when required.

- God allowed me to travel on more than forty airlines of different countries, seven luxury cruise ships, catamarans, speedboats, a sailboat, hovercraft, and so on. I also had the privilege to visit warships of the US, Britain and India, and had visited US and Indian submarines.

- I have visited and climbed on five of the six tallest buildings in the world, until the year 2000. I have also seen many tall mountains, snow mountains, erupting live volcanoes, and large waterfalls.

- One of the stars in sky, named Camelopardalis, is now known by my family name Sunny Vettimala, as allocated to me by the International Star Registry, permanently filed in the registry's vault in Switzerland. Even though I don't own this star, it is registered in my name, and it cannot be allotted to anyone else.

Now I am a US citizen living in New York. But I was born and brought up in India, with a minimum high school education. There are over a thousand million people in India now. There are many millionaires, even a few billionaires, and millions of highly qualified people. But I do not think even 1 percent of the millionaires, or these highly qualified people could achieve all I have accomplished. Therefore, I consider myself as one in a million, or one in millions, all by the grace of God.

I accepted Jesus Christ as my personal Savior and consider that as my greatest achievement in this world. Through that process, I have received citizenship in the heavenly Kingdom. I also have the promise that, even if I die, I will live again and spend eternity with my Lord and Savior Jesus Christ and His saints. Therefore, I can spend my life here, without the fear of death, but with happiness and hope.

Let me confess that none of the above-mentioned achievements are due to my educational qualifications or my hard work. It is all because of the grace, kindness, and blessings of my loving Lord and God, Jesus Christ. God also gave me the ability and mentality to complete any job allotted to me, accurately and faithfully. I had the courage and willingness to accept more responsibility, to accept changes, and to take on new challenges. I also had full confidence and faith that whenever I'm in need of help, my God will provide me enough grace to carry on that task. I even wrote this memoir by myself, even though English is not my mother tongue. It is all by the grace of God only.

It is true that all my achievements and blessings are by the grace of God. But remember that not everyone gets the same measure of blessings. So, while trusting and believing in God, we must do our part. My advice to the young generation is that we are living in a very competitive world, and higher education is very important. I had to step back from certain opportunities and events due to my lack of a degree. Don't let that happen to you.

I wish you all the best in life. All glory and honor to my Lord and Savior, Jesus Christ. Amen.